T'AO THE HERMIT

T'AO THE HERMIT

Sixty Poems by
T'ao Ch'ien
(365—427)

Translated, introduced, and annotated by
WILLIAM ACKER

THAMES AND HUDSON
LONDON · NEW YORK

All rights reserved
First published 1952

PRINTED IN GREAT BRITAIN BY
JARROLD AND SONS LTD NORWICH

TO MY MOTHER

ACKNOWLEDGMENTS

From the many who have helped me in the making of this book my especial thanks are due to the following:

To my sister, Mrs. Duncan Phillips, and to Mr. Duncan Phillips, without whose backing and encouragement I could not have undertaken it, and whose interest sustained me until its completion.

To Mr. Archibald G. Wenley, Director of the Freer Gallery of Art, Washington, D.C., for reading the translations critically and for his advice and suggestions.

To Miss Elmira Bier of the Phillips Gallery, Washington, D.C., for her help and work in preparing the manuscript.

To Mr. Frank Margesson of the Publishers, who has gone over and discussed the text with me and has made many valuable suggestions with regard to wording and phrasing, and has helped me especially in selecting the poems to be included in this book.

To Miss Deborah Stowe of Genesco, N.Y., for help in proof reading and for many valuable suggestions with regard to rhythm, wording, and phrasing.

I am greatly indebted to the various translations of Arthur Waley: to the Macmillan Company, New York, and George Allen and Unwin Ltd., London, for permission to quote from The Analects of Confucius, and to Alfred A. Knopf Inc., New York, and Constable and Company Ltd., London, for permission to include a poem from 170 Chinese Poems.

I am also indebted to a Japanese Kambun version of T'ao Ch'ien's poems by Mr. Matajiro Urushiyama which appears in the Iwanami Bunko series.

WILLIAM R. B. ACKER

CONTENTS

7

An Introduction to the Poems of T'ao Ch'ien

THE HISTORICAL BACKGROUND

T'AO CH'IEN lived in a sort of Medieval period between Classical China, the Ch'in and the Two Han dynasties on the one hand, and the cultural and political renaissance of the T'ang dynasty on the other. The Classical China of the Chou dynasty (1122–225 B.C.) had produced the great philosophers and their systems; it was an age of great freedom and originality of thought, daring speculation, earnest questioning, and fundamental doubt. The organization of the dynasty was feudal, and during its early days the Chou kings seem to have had real power over their domains; but as time went on the feudal states became in effect independent kingdoms where the different dukes, marquises, counts, and barons had their courts, their individual ancestral cults and gods of the soil, their local administrations and laws. As the central power declined, the warfare among them became more and more violent and incessant, so that in the end it became clear that peace could only come through one of the states conquering all the rest and re-establishing a central authority.

This was all the more logical, since the different states shared a common culture and the linguistic differences do not seem to have been very marked. In order to achieve such a unification, however, it was necessary to abolish once and for all the feudal nobility, ever jealous as they were of their prestige and power, and bent on perpetuating the rule of their families in their own domains.

In the west of China, the semi-barbarian state of Ch'in had been growing more and more powerful towards the end of the Chou dynasty. Its rulers had adopted the philosophy of the *fa chia* or Legalists, which amounted to a kind of Fascism with all the trimmings: youth movement, marching, singing, and the glorification of war. This warlike state finally conquered all the rest, and its first emperor, Ch'in Shih Huang Ti, ascended the throne of a united empire in 255 B.C. He abolished the hereditary nobility, changed all the feudal states into provinces and departments, unified weights and measures, simplified the system of writing, and even standardized the gauge of chariot wheels, so that his officials could travel easily to any place in the great empire. But the dynasty had spent its strength in accomplishing this vast effort of unification. Rebellions broke out among the armies, and the country was rent anew by wars, until in 206 B.C. a certain Liu Pang ascended the throne and became the first emperor of the Han dynasty.

The Han did not continue the harsh laws of the Ch'in, which were based on the Legalist philosophy, but seeking a moral basis for their government, raised Confucianism, which until then had been only one of a number of competing schools of philosophy, to the rank of official state cult; which it remained ever afterwards, with only brief intervals when certain emperors replaced it by Taoism or Buddhism. They did not restore the ancient nobility, but went even further than the Ch'in in making sure that no centres of particularism or local patriotism should arise as under the Chou. Officials were chosen in large part on the basis of character and practical ability, and partly by a system of public examinations open to all literate men. Furthermore, it became the practice to send officials to govern in other provinces than their own, and to rotate them frequently, in order to prevent them from identifying their interests with the local populations. As a result of these measures the Former Han dynasty lasted until A.D. 9; this was the year in which the usurper Wang Mang seized power and ruled until A.D. 23, when the Liu family regained the throne. Soon after this, the capital was removed from Ch'ang-an in Shensi, and a new one built at Lo-yang in Honan, the dynasty then being known as the Later Han (A.D. 25–220).

The Former and Later Han ruled the empire for more than four hundred years, protected the people from the Northern and Western barbarians in large measure, and kept the peace within its borders. When at last it weakened and fell, the empire was divided into three states, the Minor Han dynasty in the west (221–264), Wei in the north and centre, and Wu in the south and east.

But with the disappearance of the single authority of the Han and the prestige it exercised over the minds of men, any general could regard himself as the potential founder of a new dynasty, and rebellions and wars arose on every hand. In A.D. 265 the Chin dynasty arose, which ruled most of central China until 420, seven years before T'ao Ch'ien's death. It was never a strong dynasty. Most of the territory north of the Yellow River was ruled by the T'o-pa Tartars, who called their dynasty Wei; various parts of the south, west, and north-west were ruled by a number of small dynasties which rose and fell and fought with one another and the Chin with dreary monotony.

In general, the administrative system and the methods of choosing officials were the same as under the Han. Confucianism was still the official state religion, but Buddhism, first introduced into China during the Han dynasty, had taken root and flourished, while Taoism had begun to organize itself into a Church and build temples and shrines in imitation of Buddhism.

But it was an unhappy time compared to the great Han dynasty. Continual warfare with rebels and other states to the north and west drained the resources of the people, as did also the corrupt and lax officials to whom the Chin emperors set

13

anything but a shining example. The dynasty did not produce a single emperor of high character or outstanding ability.

However, the arts flourished, largely under the patronage of the great Buddhist temples which were decorated with fine wall paintings and cult images. Magnificent pagodas and halls were built everywhere, and the sacred books were often illustrated by the learned monks who copied them. Handwriting, too, had come to be regarded as a fine art equal or superior to painting, and the greatest calligrapher in all Chinese history was Wang Hsi-chih (321-379), an elder contemporary of T'ao Ch'ien. Ku K'ai-chih, one of China's most renowned painters, was also his contemporary, his dates being approximately 345 to 411. These men were literary figures as well, but T'ao Ch'ien does not seem to have known either of them.

Classical China had not paid much attention to art. Music was highly developed, but was chiefly used in the court rituals, though scholars and literary men played on the *ch'in*; this was a flat instrument resembling a lute or zither, which the player placed before him on the floor or on a low table, since the Chinese did not begin to use chairs until Sung times. Handwriting was regarded primarily as a practical accomplishment, and only later under the Han and Chin, rose to the status of a fine art. Painting is scarcely mentioned in the Chou literature, and it is evident that the painter must have been regarded as merely one kind of artisan among others. Even literature was not treated as an art in the same degree as later: the emphasis was more on content than on style, and most of the prose works were concerned with philosophy, history, ritual, and such matters. Poetry existed and was prized, but—at any rate in the Confucian school—almost more for its content and instructive value than for its beauty. Confucius, for example, urges his disciples to study the ancient *Book of Songs* (*Shih Ching*):

The Master said, Let a man be first incited by the *Songs*,

then given a firm footing by the study of ritual, and finally perfected by music. (Waley, *Analects*, VIII, 8.)

And again:

The Master said, Little ones, Why is it that none of you study the *Songs*? For the *Songs* will help you to incite people's emotions, to observe their feelings, to keep company, to express your grievances. They may be used at home in the service of one's father; abroad, in the service of one's prince. Moreover, they will widen your acquaintance with the names of birds, beasts, plants, and trees.

(Waley, *Analects*, XVII, 9.)

The *Book of Songs* is certainly the best preserved of all the ancient Chinese texts, and much of it may be considerably older than Confucius' time (traditional dates 551–479 B.C.). It is an anthology of three hundred songs and poems from the various feudal states. Some are pure folk-songs, love songs, songs of courtship and marriage, songs to be sung at village dances, and so on; others, less "folk" in character, are laments and complaints about the hardships of war, official service, and the like, or eulogies of a prince or patron.

Many of them have the same fresh charm as the best British, French, or German folk-songs, and no student of comparative folk-lore could possibly mistake their character. Yet it is evident that even in the Chou dynasty many mistook their original nature and purpose, saw all sorts of morals and political allegories in even the simplest of them; a neglected lover would be understood as a minister out of favour at court, the beloved as a prince, and so on. The *Tso Chuan*, an extended commentary on the *Spring and Autumn Annals* of the state of Lu from the year 721 to 481 B.C., abounds in passages in which feudal lords quote the *Songs* to one another at ceremonious meetings, vying with one another in the choice of quotations containing meanings which they deemed apt according to acquired interpretations. This view of the *Shih Ching* held the field throughout Chinese history, and was shared by the earlier European translators such as Couvreur and Legge. It remained for Marcel Granet in his *Fêtes et Chansons Anciennes de la Chine* (Paris, 1919) to point out the true character of the ancient poems, and let them stand before us as they really are. Arthur Waley has made an excellent translation of them into English, also dispensing, like Granet, with the endless political allusions, identifications, veiled metaphors, and morals which the early Confucian commentators saw, or thought they saw, in them.

But history is just as much the study of what people thought was true as it is of what was in fact true, and T'ao Ch'ien no doubt accepted the official Confucian view of the *Songs*. It is all the more fortunate that he does not allude to them very much; indeed, if he had done so, while believing in the theories of the commentators, he could not possibly have written such fresh and spontaneous verse as he did.

CHINESE POETRY FROM THE 'BOOK OF SONGS' TO T'AO CH'IEN

As we have seen, the three hundred poems of the *Book of Songs* were known to Confucius, and probably in pretty much their present form. They owe their preservation to the fact that, because he so often urged the study of them upon his disciples, they came to be regarded as sacred scripture by the scholars of the Confucian school—indeed, until quite recently most Confucians held that he had collected and compiled them himself, along with the *Classic of History*, the *Book of Rites*, and other texts of the canon.

It was otherwise with the whole body of ancient poetry which must have existed over and above the three hundred poems of this anthology; except for minor fragments no poems in the four-word metre were collected and preserved after its compilation until Ch'in and Han times. However, towards the end of the Chou dynasty a new sort of poem appeared with lines of varying length, the lines being frequently broken by a sort of interjection—*hsi*—similar in its effect to "Oh" as found in such a verse as:

> There were three gypsies a come to my door
> And downstairs ran this a lady Oh,
> One sang high, the other sang low
> And another sang bonny bonny Biscay Oh.

The following literal translation of the first four lines of the "Elegiac[1] Poem on the Autumn Wind" will serve to illustrate the nature of the metre.

Ch'iu	Autumn
feng	wind
ch'i	rise
hsi—	hey—
pai	white
yün	cloud
fei	fly
Ts'ao	Grass
mu	tree
huang	yellow
lo	fall
hsi—	hey—

[1] Poems in this irregular metre, characterized by the use of *hsi*, are usually called elegiac poems in English.

yen	wild-goose
nan	south
kuei	return
Lan	Orchid
yu	have
hsiu	elegance
hsi—	hey—
chü	chrysanthemum
yu	have
fang	fragrance
Huai	Cherish
chia	lovely
jen	person
hsi—	hey—
pu	not
neng	can
wang	forget

The best compositions in this metre were the *Ch'u tz'u* or *Elegies of Ch'u*, the work of a school of poets who flourished in the great southern feudal state of Ch'u during the last hundred years or so before it fell to the Ch'in in 225 B.C. The greatest of these poets was Ch'ü Yüan (332–295 B.C.) whose *Li Sao* or *Sorrows of Exile* is one of the masterpieces of Chinese literature.[1]

The *Ch'u tz'u* were generally rather long, and characterized by an impetuous flow of wildly luxuriant verbiage, giving an effect of great vehemence and passion. To them the word *shih* —"poem"—is never applied, but many shorter compositions in this metre are loosely called *shih* in the anthologies of *ku shih*— "old poems"—such as the *Ku Shih Yüan* (*Fountain of Old*

[1] Arthur Waley has made a beautiful translation of one of his poems, "Battle", in *170 Chinese Poems*.

Poems) and the *Ku Shih Shang Hsi* (*Old Poems Criticized and Explained*).

Before going any further I should make it plain that, for the purposes of this book, when I use the words poem or poetry I refer only to what the Chinese call by the name *shih*; that is, relatively short rhymed compositions, mostly with uniform lines of four or five characters each (but including some in the elegiac metre and a few of seven words per line) and mainly of lyric content, though purely narrative or didactic *shih* also occur. I emphasize this because, besides the *Ch'u Tz'u*, another type of composition which is a kind of poetry, flourished through-out the late Chou, Ch'in, and especially during the Han dynasty, as well as during the period of the Three Kingdoms. I refer to the *fu*, a word which approximates to our "prose-poem". They are unrhymed, and have lines of irregular length. As a rule these compositions are translated as prose, but the style is frequently so lofty that they are suitable for rendering into blank verse. In any case, whether we consider them as prose-poems or poetic prose, they represent literary art of a very high order, and were the chief vehicle of artistic literary expression during the Han dynasty.

But to return to four-word poems: even to Confucius and his disciples some of the vocabulary and grammar of the *Book of Songs* seems not to have been altogether clear and familiar,[1] and by the beginning of the Han dynasty these poems must have seemed definitely archaic when read aloud. Most of the *Songs* are four-word poems (*ssu yen shih*)—poems in which each line, with occasional exceptions, consists of four characters only—and no doubt during the remainder of the Chou and Ch'in dynasties, and well into the Han period, except for poems in the elegiac metre most of the verse that was composed was in this four-word rhythm. During the Former Han dynasty, however, five-word poems (*wu yen shih*) began to be

[1] cf. Waley, *Analects*, II, 2, and note 1.

written; while, by the middle of the Later Han (25 B.C. to A.D. 22), five-word poems were the rule, a poet using four-word metre as a rule only when he was consciously trying to imitate the *Book of Songs* or to write in an archaic or solemn style. T'ao Ch'ien, too, wrote a number of four-word poems, five of which are included in this book (pp. 135–147). In them he has tried to emulate the antique phraseology and grammar, and in general they have a more serious and solemn air about them than we find in his five-word poems.[1] This is because, writing in an age when it was no longer in popular use, the minute he tried his hand at this metre he was bound to be influenced by the enormous prestige of the ancient classic, resulting in a certain constraint on spontaneity. I think the difference should be apparent even in my translations.

The five-word poems of the Later Han were, with few exceptions, not of high artistic quality. Most of them were in the nature of ballads and lyrics intended to be sung at banquets, and a collection of these was made by the palace *yo fu* or Music Bureau, the name *yo fu* being then applied to the whole body of such material.

Perhaps the best of the very early examples of five-word verse are contained in the group of Nineteen Old Poems, seventeen of which have been translated by Arthur Waley (*170 Chinese Poems*) and which, as he says, had an enormous influence on all subsequent Chinese poetry, T'ao Ch'ien's being no exception.

Perhaps the first writers of real ability to elevate the five-word poem to a place beside the *fu* as a means of serious artistic self-expression were the poets of the remarkable Ts'ao family. Ts'ao Ts'ao (A.D. 155–220) figured largely in the struggles attending the break-up of the Han dynasty. His name is still known to every Chinese as a general of all but supernatural brilliance and energy ("speak of Ts'ao Ts'ao—Ts'ao Ts'ao has already

[1] He never used the elegiac metre.

20

arrived"), but he was also a literatus and a poet. His son, Ts'ao P'ei, became the first Emperor of Wei of the Three Kingdoms, and ruled from 220 to 227 as Wen Ti. He gave his father the posthumous title of Wu Ti (Warrior Emperor). He was a good poet, but was far excelled both in *fu* and *shih* by his younger brother, Ts'ao Chih (A.D. 192–232), whom he hated because their father had several times thought of naming him heir-apparent.[1] The story goes that when Ts'ao P'ei ascended the throne, he sought to trap his brother by requiring him to compose a poem in the time required to walk seven paces, or die. Ts'ao Chih at once composed the following while taking the seven steps:

> When you boil beans
> By burning their own stalks
> The beans will weep
> Even in the Pot.
> Verily they grew
> From the same root—
> Why should they hasten
> To burn their brothers?

But this is scarcely a fair example of his poetry composed under less trying circumstances. He probably did more than any other poet until T'ao Ch'ien to make the five-word poem a great medium of artistic expression.[2]

The Chin dynasty which followed the Three Kingdoms succeeded in unifying most of central China, holding it together in spite of incessant warfare with the Tartars to the north and a number of small kingdoms to the west and north-west. From A.D. 265 to 316 the capital was at Lo-yang, with

---

[1] For translations of poems by Ts'ao P'ei and Ts'ao Chih, see Waley, *170 Chinese Poems*.

[2] Ts'ao Jui, a son of Ts'ao P'ei who ruled as Ming Ti from A.D. 227 to 240, also wrote some verse, but nothing to compare with the other three.

a secondary capital at Ch'ang-an in Shensi; but as the power of the dynasty waned, as so often in Chinese history, it became necessary to move the capital eastwards to a place less accessible to the marauding Tartars. The place chosen was Chien-yeh, the modern Nanking, which remained the capital from 317 till 419. It was not very far down the Yang-tzu from Hsün-yang, the modern Kiukiang, near which T'ao Ch'ien had his home. T'ao Ch'ien's life thus falls within the period of Chinese history known as the Eastern Chin dynasty, except for the last seven years spent under the reigns of the Emperors Wu (420–423), Shao (423) and Wen (424–454) of the Liu Sung dynasty, which succeeded the Chin in the south.

The Chin dynasty poets who preceded T'ao Ch'ien were all far beneath him in style and content. Fu Hsüan (died A.D. 278)[1] wrote graceful, melancholy verse, especially about the sorrows of women:

> Far, far your chariot O,
>   vigorous your steeds,
> My thoughts follow you O,
>   I can not forget,
> Lightly you travel O,
>   westwards to Ch'in.
> Would I were your shadow O,
>   to go by your side.
> If you'd be in the shade O,
>   the shadow'd disappear,
> That you stay in the sun O
>   is all that I'd desire.

Further worthy of mention are P'an Yao (died A.D. 300), Lu Chi (261–303), Tso Ssu (died c. 306)[2], Kiu K'un (270–317), Kuo P'u (276–324), and Yang Fang (died c. 319). All

[1] Two of his poems, "A Gentle Wind" and "Woman", are in Waley's *170 Chinese Poems*.
[2] ibid.

22

of these wrote good verse, but T'ao Ch'ien shows very little of
their influence, since his poems are to such an outstanding
degree the direct expression of his own temperament and
personality.

T'AO CH'IEN'S BIOGRAPHY

THE BARE bones of T'ao Ch'ien's life are recorded in almost
the same form in three of the Dynastic Histories. These dynastic
histories of China, whose compilation was entrusted to well-
known literati as an honour as well as a salaried employment,
consist very largely of biographies of distinguished men, states-
men, generals, scholars, or any whose lives seemed worthy of
recording. The biographies were given separate classifications,
such as Loyal Ministers, Rebellious Officials, Filial Sons,
Great Confucian Scholars, etc., but T'ao Ch'ien was put in
a rather strange category—that of *yin i*—the "hidden and aloof". ⌒
These seem to have been people of great ability, men whose
gifts were so great that they should by rights have played a
significant rôle in their age, but who because of some unfortu-
nate trait of character or some strange idiosyncrasy could not
bring their great talents to bear in a practical way.

The following contains the gist of what the histories have
to say:[1]

T'ao Ch'ien, courtesy title Yüan-ming.[2] A man of
Ch'ai-sang near Hsün-yang [the modern Kiukiang]. One

---

[1] Taken from the *Wen hsüeh chia ta t'zu tien*. Slightly condensed.

[2] It is interesting that two of his names seem to refer to his character of hermit.
T'ao, of course, was his surname. Ch'ien means to be hidden in the depths, to
lurk unseen, especially under water. The courtesy title or style was a name given
by friends on coming of age. *Yüan* means "abyss", and *ming* "light" or "brilliance", so that Yüan-ming, his courtesy title, would mean "Light of the Abyss".
Yüan-liang has the same meaning, *liang* being another word for "bright",
"brilliance", etc.

23

source says that his given name was Yüan‑ming and his courtesy title Yüan‑liang. In his youth he was pure and high‑minded: he was widely read and excelled in literary composition. He was aristocratically off‑hand in his demeanour and unconstrained in manner. He relied upon the Real and was self‑contained, so that his neighbours and fellow‑townsmen thought highly of him. He once wrote the *Story of the Master of the Five Willows* in order to render an account of himself.

Since his parents were old and his family poor, he was recommended for, and accepted the post of Libationer for his district. But he could not bear official service and after a short time resigned and went home. Next, the province offered him a position as Keeper of Records, but he would not accept it. He ploughed in person and provided for himself, until in the end he suffered starvation and illness. Later he was summoned to be Adjutant to the Chien‑wei Garrison Commander, whereupon he wrote to an intimate friend, saying: "Is it right that I should rather wish to play and sing to keep up the 'three short‑cuts'?"[1] When one of his superiors heard of this he saw to it that he was given the position of Governor of Peng‑tse. In his official capacity he ordered that all the public lands of the District be sown with glutinous millet [suitable for brewing wine] "which should be just enough to keep me drunk with wine". When however, his wife and children begged that he should have some land sown with plain millet, he had a hundred and fifty acres sown with glutinous millet and fifty sown with plain millet.

---

[1] "A certain Chiang Hsü made three short‑cuts through the bamboos around his house and only his intimates Ch'in‑chung and Yang‑chung used them to come to visit him. . . ." From this the term "three short‑cuts" has the meaning of a hermit's abode. T'ao Ch'ien means that he would rather earn money in the low capacity of hired entertainer than as a military adviser.

By nature he was plain and honest and never used his office to his private advantage. When the provincial government sent a Censor to his district, all the other officials went to pay their respects to him arrayed in their best, but he merely sighed and said: "How can I bend my waist for five pecks of rice and earnestly pay court to such a yokel!" In the second year of the I Hsi era [A.D. 406] he gave up his seal of office and returned to his home, and thereupon wrote his famous prose-poem "I am on my Way Home",[1] in order to make his intentions clear. Later he was offered a post as Drafter of Official Documents, but refused it. After that he spent all his time with his friends Chang Yeh, Chou Hsüan-jen, Yang Sung-ling, Ch'ung Tsun and others. Sometimes when he had wine he would invite them, or he would ask them to go with him to some party where wine was being served. Even if he did not know the host at all, he would enjoy himself with the utmost gaiety and not return home till he was drunk. At other times when friends went to his house with wine and a prepared feast, he would have nothing whatever to say. But (usually) whenever he got drunk he would become as one inspired and make incredible conversational hits.

Also, he had no heart for making a living and left management of his household entirely to his children and servants. Whatever they did, he never showed approbation or disapprobation: only, if there was wine he would drink it; if there was none he would still go on humming verses to himself incessantly. He once playfully gave himself the name of *Hsi Huang Shang jen*.[2]

By nature he did not understand notes, and yet he treas-ured a lute which had no strings. Every time friends came

---

[1] One of the most famous prose-poems in Chinese literature.

[2] Hsi Huang is another name for Fu Hsi, first of the Divine Sages—culture heroes of antiquity. *Shang jen* is a Buddhist term meaning adept.

and wine was served, he would take it in his hands and caress it, saying "all I care about is the meaning within the lute; why should I bother with the notes upon the strings?"

Of works by him there are preserved ten chapters of poetry. There are also preserved ten chapters of a work called *Later Records on Research into Spiritual Matters* which does nothing but record strange and wonderful matters. It is, everything considered, the work of a forger, but it is still extant.

These are, in the main, the facts that the histories relate concerning him. The dynastic historiographers duly took note of his dates of birth and death, his meagre official career, and certain anecdotes—his occasional appearance at parties to which he had not been invited, his stringless lute, etc. Of his literary work they say only that "he was widely read, and excelled in literary composition", and mention his *Story of the Master of the Five Willows* and his famous prose-poem "I am on my Way Home", of which they give the complete text.[1] It is perhaps asking too much of them to expect that they should have hailed him as China's greatest poet to date in the five-word metre. I think that T'ao Ch'ien himself, like Horace, took his own measure and was quietly certain that his poems would stand the test of time, and that he had this in mind when he wrote:

> Renouncing my cap of office
> I will return to my old home
> Never more entangled
> with love for high position.
> I will nourish my REAL self
> under my gates and thatch
> And by doing this
> be all the better known.[2]

[1] I hope to bring out a translation of this and other of his prose-poems in a subsequent volume. [2] See p. 110.

THE STORY OF THE MASTER
OF THE FIVE WILLOWS

IN THE following short composition with eulogy T'ao Ch'ien gives us an idealized view of himself as he might have wished posterity to remember him:

The Master's place of origin is not known, nor are his surname and given name anywhere recorded, but beside his house were five willow trees from which he took this pseudonym. Quiet, silent, and of few words, he did not strive for gain or glory. He loved to read, but did not care whether he understood everything completely. When he did have an insight into the meaning [of a passage] he would be so happy that he would forget to eat.

By nature he was fond of wine, but his household was poor and he could not always get it. His intimates and friends, knowing how it was with him, would sometimes lay in a supply and invite him. Once he began to drink, he would finish each cup quickly, his one thought being to get drunk without fail. And once he was drunk he would simply retire, without ever feeling embarrassed about whether to stay or leave.

The enclosure around his house was desolate and neglected, and did not keep out the wind and sun. His short coat of hempen cloth was worn and patched, his rice chest and wine gourd were often empty, yet he was ever serene of heart. He constantly wrote for his own amusement, and thereby also revealed his mind. He was utterly unconcerned with success or failure and so lived out his days.

His eulogy says:

Ch'ien Lou[1] had a saying—
"Fret not at being poor and humble,
Strive not for riches and nobility."

If one carries this saying
To the ultimate conclusion,
Is one any longer
A common mortal?
He was merry with the cup
And wrote his poems
To please his mind.
Was he not a subject
Of the sage Without-desire?
Was he not a subject
Of the Emperor Ko-t'ien?[2]

T'AO CH'IEN'S LIFE AND CHARACTER AS REVEALED IN HIS POEMS

HIS POVERTY

IN HIS poems T'ao Ch'ien frequently calls attention to his poverty and his ability to "endure adversity", but it is obvious that we should not take "poverty" to mean anything like utter destitution. His was by no means the poverty of the ordinary unlettered peasant, or the ordinary labourer in the fields. It is merely that he considered himself poor for a member of his standing and most particularly for a man of his talents and abilities. For a man of his class there were, practically speaking, only two ways in which to be comfortably situated: a successful government career, or land ownership on a large scale. Trade

---

[1] See p. 130 (one of the poor scholars of that series).

[2] A mythical Sage Emperor of remote antiquity who "did not speak and believed in himself; did not (seek to) change things and acted spontaneously".

or business or manufacturing were looked down upon to such an extent that it would have been impossible for a man like him to engage in them, even had he wished to do so.

The business of the government was carried on in the classical written language which one must have mastered to obtain even the humblest civil post, and since the drafting of memorials to the throne, decrees, edicts, petitions and all important official documents required literary ability of a high order, such ability was usually a sure means to wealth and power. With his gifts T'ao Ch'ien should have had a brilliant career in the government, perhaps even at court; but as the biographers point out, "he could not bear official service", and never kept any post for long. This was due, perhaps, to a stubborn refusal to make the necessary compromises demanded of anyone who wished to rise quickly in office; he would not cultivate the right people if they did not happen to appeal to him, he would not associate with those who bored or irritated him, or even be polite to them. Even to his friends he could be very blunt. One of the biographies relates that when guests came to his house to drink with him, as soon as he was drunk he would simply say "I am drunk and wish to sleep, you had better go now."

But if he found the protocol and etiquette of official life intolerable, most of his colleagues, on their part, no doubt found him uncouth and rude—impossible, in fact. And, if the truth were known, his drinking may have seriously interfered with his competence as an official.

Accordingly, since he could not have a career in government service, and any kind of trade would have been unthinkable for a literatus such as he was, there was nothing for him to do but stay on his land and farm it himself. He seems to have lived in a fairly comfortable house:

> My land and house—
> a little more than ten acres,

29

> In the thatched cottage—
>> only eight or nine rooms.
> Elms and willows
>> shade the back verandah,
> Peach and plum trees
>> in rows before the hall.[1]

"Eight or nine rooms" does not sound so small to a modern ear and does not seem to go with poverty, but it must be remembered that some, at least, of his children and their families shared the house with him, not to mention the servants. There seems to have been a court with buildings all around it and shaded with trees.

His biographies tell us that he practically left the management of the household and farm entirely to his children and the servants. Perhaps if he had really put his mind to supervising the work on his estate he need not have been so poor. Nevertheless, I feel certain that he really loved his land and at times of ploughing, sowing, and reaping went out and worked himself, or at least superintended the work in person.

Starvation and hunger are often mentioned in the poems. I doubt if he ever really starved in the literal sense; it seems more likely that in lean years the grain had to be carefully rationed so that it should last until the next harvest, and everybody in the household had to share and share alike a very meagre diet, but one sufficient to maintain life and a degree of health.

> I have never yet
>> utterly failed my family
> Even though cold and hungry
>> they always had bran and gruel.[2]

The poem "On Going to Take in the Harvest at the Outlying Farm at Hsiasun" is interesting in that it describes a sort

[1] See p. 52.   [2] See p. 78.

of expedition, with a party of his field-hands, to do the harvesting on land that he owned at some distance from that on which his house stood. He was thus definitely a landowner, and may have owned several such outlying plots or farms; but this is the only one mentioned in the poems, except perhaps the "Southern Acres" mentioned in a poem written in 403, which seems to refer to a trip to inspect some land that he owned:

> Long ago I heard of the Southern Acres,
> But in those years I never really trod them.
> Since it is possible to be "often hungry"
> Labours of spring may not be avoided.
> At the first light of dawn I harnessed my chariot—
> No sooner had I started than my thoughts were there
>   before me.[1]

And while at the "Southern Acres" he evidently superintended the ploughing and sowing, for in the sequel to this poem we find:

> Holding the plough, I rejoice in the season's labours,
> And with jokes and laughter encourage my fellow
>   workers.
> The level fields receive and welcome the wind from far,
> And healthy sprouts thrill at the spring's return.
> Although it is too soon to estimate the harvest
> Going about my work I am glad of many things. . . .

No, T'ao Ch'ien was not poor in the absolute sense. I think that a careful reading of his poems should convince anyone that he was a sort of country gentleman or gentleman farmer, and a landowner in a modest way. His poverty, such as it was, was entirely due to his own indifference alike to the management of his lands and to his antipathy to official life.

> It was all in *me*, how could I blame Heaven?

[1] See p. 112.

T'AO THE HERMIT

T'AO CH'IEN is often referred to in Chinese literature as T'ao yin-chü—T'ao the Dweller-in-Hiding, or T'ao the Hermit, and in his poems he likes to compare himself to Ch'ang-chü and Chieh-ni[1] and to the Old Man with the Staff[2]—all recluses mentioned in the *Analects of Confucius*, who criticized the Master for his ceaseless striving to convert and change the world and make the Way of the Ancient Sage Kings prevail again on earth. These were hermits on philosophical grounds who really scorned the world and all official life, but I do not think that T'ao Ch'ien was such a type at all. There is too much talk of drinking and feasting with friends, congenial gatherings, picnics and excursions, for that to have been so. We know from his biographies that he was incorruptible in office, which he never used for private gain, and no doubt he was disgusted by the venality and rapaciousness of many of his colleagues. Yet one gains the impression that he was the sort of man who would have been more shocked by vulgarity than by dishonesty. There are no outbursts of indignation against officialdom as he found it; one senses only a sort of aloofness. He simply reserved the right not to be venal or self-serving, and not to associate with those he considered vulgar. Hence there is nothing dour or fanatical about his hermitship. It must be remembered, too, that he did after all accept a number of posts that were offered him, and chose to renounce ambition for the distinguished career to which his abilities, taken by themselves, should have entitled him, entirely on the basis of accurate self-knowledge gained by experience:

[1] See p. 123 and note 3.   [2] See p. 112 and note 2.

Even if I could learn
                to follow the curb and reins,
To go against one's nature
                is always a mistake.[1]

He had a profound love for his land and the country life—
genuine and deeply felt—but, quite naturally too, a sense of
sorrow at the waste of the talents which he knew he possessed,
and which could have been used to advantage by the dynasty
had not other aspects of his character made it impossible.

HIS DRINKING

T'ao Ch'ien wrote a great many poems in praise of wine—
poems on drinking alone at home:

My chrysanthemums in autumn
                have a glorious colour,
I pluck the blossoms
                while they are wet with dew.
Floating with this thing
                that can banish sorrow
My feelings are transported
                and leave the world behind.
Raising a wine cup
                I empty it alone.
When the cup is empty
                the jug tips of itself . . .[2]

and poems on drinking with friends:

Some of my friends
                who share my taste
Arrive in a body
                carrying jugs of wine.

[1] See p. 67.   [2] From a poem not included in this book.

Parting the bushes
    we sit beneath the pine.
After several cupfuls—
    already drunk again.
Fathers and elders
    talk and chat at random—
The toasts and pledges
    lose their proper sequence.
When one does not even know
    that the self exists,
How shall one know
    that things are to be valued?[1]

If these by themselves do not necessarily lead us to the conclusion that he was an alcoholic, the poem "On Stopping Wine"[2] leaves no doubt at all. Anyone who has had any experience with alcoholism does not need to be told what ruin it can cause in the life of the sufferer and of those dependent on him:

Since then from day to day
    I have never stopped wine,
For if I stopped it
    my feelings knew no pleasure.
Stopping at evening
    I could not get to sleep,
Stopping at dawn
    I could not even rise.

What an accurate description of the terrible vicious circle in which the alcoholic, as distinct from the normal user or even the heavy drinker, becomes helplessly involved! And how characteristic the hopeless bewilderment and despair expressed in the following lines:

[1] From a poem not included in this book.   [2] p. 70.

>   Yet from day to day
>   I have wished to stop.
>   When all my hopes and plans
>   stopped, and did not thrive.
>   All that I knew
>   was that stopping was a hardship,
>   And never could believe
>   stopping could profit me.

"Stopped and did not thrive"! Perhaps we need look no further
for the cause of his failure in official life, although heavy drinking was not only condoned but expected in the social life of the
time, including official banquets and entertainments. But there
is a vast difference between even very heavy drinking—a conscious self-indulgence which can be stopped at will—and
alcoholism which is neurotic and compulsive, and rarely
amenable to control by the will or reason.

>   At last having understood
>   that it were well to stop,
>   This very morning
>   I have really stopped.
>   And now, henceforward,
>   from this stopping on,
>   I shall be stopping
>   on the shores of Fairyland.
>   My clear visage
>   will stop the morning-after face,
>   And may this never stop
>   for a hundred thousand years!

The degree of anguish and desperate desire to stop drinking for
good which he must have been feeling when he wrote this poem
is reflected in the fact that the word "stop" occurs in every line
of it, a circumstance which makes it all but impossible to
translate it with much grace; but I include it in this book

because of the light it throws on this affliction, which must have been one of the chief causes of his poverty and other hardships.

Alcoholism will sometimes yield to the power of a religious conversion or a deeply felt spiritual experience as the Alcoholics Anonymous have shown in our time. Let us hope that this poem was the result of such a dynamic episode in his spiritual life, and that he really succeeded in stopping. But if it was merely the expression of a desperate hope or an attempt to use will-power, we can be sure that he was soon drinking again. We cannot know, and can only surmise, since his biographers leave us in the dark.

HIS PHILOSOPHICAL VIEWS

T'ao Ch'ien's philosophy—his *Weltanschauung*—was entirely native Chinese and preponderantly Confucian. Nowhere in the poems is there any mention of Buddhism or any allusion to Indian doctrines or beliefs such as transmigration, rebirth in other worlds or heavens, *nirvāna*, Bodhisattvahood. Nor is there any mention of Buddhist temples or monks and priests; and this is strange, since Buddhism with its temples and monasteries was everywhere, and every Chinese must have known something about its doctrines. T'ao Ch'ien seems merely to have ignored all this, perhaps objecting to it because of its foreign origin; and though he called himself a hermit, he probably had a temperamental dislike of monkhood and the ideal of celibacy. The fact that Buddhism disapproves of drinking and meat eating may also have given him an aversion to it.

He mentions Taoism, but with mild expressions of doubt concerning its claims that one can become an Immortal through the practice of the Taoist *yoga* and sexual regimen, feeding upon rare herbs and dew, avoidance of grain and the like:

> I have no art
>> To soar and be transfigured;
> That it must be so
>> I cannot ever question.[1]

And elsewhere:

> That our destined life
>> is all too soon exhausted;
> From olden time
>> men have been saying this.
> Once in this world
>> there were Sung and Ch'iao,
> But what do we hear for certain
>> of such men nowadays?[2]

Sung is short for Ch'ih Sung-tzu and Ch'iao for Wang Tzu-ch'iao, both Taoist Immortals of legendary fame. Perhaps T'ao Ch'ien half believed that such men had once existed, but he plainly did not believe that any of his contemporaries became Immortals in the same manner.

The poem "Substance, Shadow and Spirit" contains a clear account of his attitude towards life and particularly death, ending as it does with the words:

> When it is time to go
>> then we should simply go.
> There is nothing after all
>> that we can do about it.[3]

And elsewhere,

> The life of man is like a shadow-play
> Which must in the end return to nothingness.[4]

[1] p. 46. [2] From a poem not included in this book.
[3] p. 48. [4] p. 56.

And again,

> How can we know what happens
>> once we are dead and gone?
> To suit our own heart
>> *that* good alone is certain.
> The traveller feeds his body
>> as if worth a thousand gold:
> When he approaches Change
>> his treasure melts away.[1]

From these passages, and many more which the reader will notice in the poems, it is clear that T'ao Ch'ien did not believe in the sort of personal immortality which was the avowed ideal of the Taoist of his day. What is more, even if he believed that sincere Taoist adepts might once have found the elixir of life, or that by means of other esoteric practices they succeeded in becoming Immortals and now lived in the fairyland of P'eng-lai in the midst of the Eastern ocean or on the summits of the sacred mountains such as Sung-shan and Hua-shan or the K'un-lun range, he doubted that there were any who could do it now. And, finally, he frankly did not care whether they did so or not; at any rate he himself was quite uninterested in the whole question of immortality or becoming an Immortal:

> Becoming an Immortal
>> is a steep and dangerous road
> But to set one's own ideals
>> is a broad and level highway.
> If we are lofty
>> in our everyday pursuits
> What would be the use
>> of climbing Hua or Sung.[2]

He thus scorns the whole goal of popular Taoism, though he had no doubt read the ancient philosophical texts, the *Tao*

[1] From a poem not included in this book.   [2] p. 88.

Te Ching attributed to Lao Tzu, and the *Chuang Tzu*, neither of which speaks much of Immortals or lays any stress on survival even in a purified form, feeding upon air and dew. So, when he uses the terms Tao (the Way) and *chen* (the Real) they undoubtedly have some of the meaning they have in Taoist philosophy.

In general, however, the word Tao means the Way of the *Analects of Confucius*, the Way which the Master believed had once prevailed upon earth, and which he hoped would prevail again.

In "Substance, Shadow, and Spirit" we find an ancient Chinese conception of the components of the human being, which was pretty generally shared by all the ancient philosophers. According to this primitive system of thought, man has a body (substance), a material soul (shadow), and an ethereal soul (spirit). The material soul which T'ao Ch'ien calls shadow, and identifies with the visible shadow cast by the sun, was supposed to cling to the body and hover about the grave after death—a sort of swirl of psychic energy in the locality, which might give rise to gross manifestations such as spiritualistic phenomena, "ghosts", etc. In time, it became utterly dispersed and died. The ethereal soul (spirit), which T'ao Ch'ien more or less identifies with the intelligence, does not remain with the body but rises to inhabit some higher sphere, if not for ever, then at least for a far longer time than the shadow should survive. But the thought of this survival seems to give T'ao Ch'ien no comfort at all. It is as though he felt that the human personality could be interesting only so long as the three components were still united:

> All the things that make us
>   care about our lives—
> They are surely compassed
>   within a single lifetime.[1]

[1] p. 65.

In all this he shows himself a true Confucian: did not the Master reply to a disciple who asked about death, "When you do not know about life, how can you know about death?" And do not the *Analects* tell us that "The Master never talked of prodigies, feats of strength, disorders, or spirits"?

Of all the quotations and literary allusions in the poems, the overwhelming majority are to the *Analects* which T'ao Ch'ien must have loved above all other books. The only thing which might give one to pause is his fondness for identifying himself with the hermit-philosophers Ch'ang-chü and Chieh-ni, and the Old Man with the Staff,[1] all rather dour people who made it plain that they held Confucius in some contempt for being so active—travelling about from state to state seeking some prince who might employ him and give him a chance to try out his theories and help bring the world back to the Way. Probably they too might have admitted that the world had once been perfect, that the Way had once prevailed, but they did not think it was up to them to try to restore it, nor did they think it the business of any individual, however wise. They had heard of Confucius, and no doubt conceded his learning and noble purpose; what they decried and ridiculed was his ceaseless activity, his unquenchable hope of accomplishing something in his own lifetime. It was, of course, a matter of temperament. Confucius was the sort of man who had to go on actively striving to bring the world a little closer to perfection, even though no one knew better than he how unlikely he was to succeed. Consider *Analects*, XIV, 41:

Tzu-lu was spending the night at the Stone Gates. The gate-keeper said, Where are you from? Tzu-lu said, From Master K'ung's. The man said, He's the one who knows it's no use, but keeps on doing it, is that not so?

[1] The quotations from the *Analects* in which they appear are given in full in footnotes on pp. 113, 114, and 124.

Some consider that the passages in the *Analects* in which the Master is represented as being criticized or even snubbed by recluses must be accretions drawn from sources unfriendly to him, quietists especially; but I do not think that this is necessarily so. I think it more likely that Confucius understood such people quite well, and sincerely regretted it when they refused to meet him or talk to him.

After all, there are many passages in the *Analects* which stress the impropriety of remaining in office when the Tao does not prevail, not to mention serving under a corrupt or wicked prince. And T'ao Ch'ien could always cite the following passage, which I quote from Waley's translation (XIV, 39), together with his note:

> The Master said, Best of all, to withdraw from one's generation; next, to withdraw to another land; next, to leave because of a look; next best, to leave because of a word.

Waley explains this passage in the following words:

> If *Tao* (the Way) does not prevail, it is better to flee altogether from the men of one's generation, rather than to go round "perching first here, then there" as Confucius himself had unsuccessfully done, or to wait till the expression of a ruler's face betrays that he is meditating some enormity; or worst of all, to wait till his words actually reveal his intention.

There seems no reason to reject this saying because Confucius did not in fact "withdraw from his generation" and become a hermit. No doubt he often felt like it, and a few passages describe him as wanting to settle among the barbarians[1] to get

[1] Waley, *Analects*, v, 6, and ix, 13.

41

away from it all; but like Socrates he had some daemon within him which compelled him to go on trying though he knew that it was useless.

At all events the existence of such passages in the *Analects* excuses T'ao Ch'ien, who was evidently an enthusiastic Confucian, from trying in every way to emulate the Master; they explain, too, why he saw no inconsistency in quoting from the *Analects* at every turn and yet feeling kinship with hermit-philosophers who had all but insulted Confucius. It is as though T'ao Ch'ien had said: "The Master had both tendencies within him: he understood them, but they in their narrowness, being smaller men, did not understand him. While I honour him for continuing to strive against hopeless odds, when it comes to this one question of public service, I must range myself on their side. Besides, perhaps the world is in an even worse way now than it was in his time. Who knows, perhaps if he were alive and with us now, even he would give it up for lost and be a hermit too." Such, in effect, I believe was his attitude, or his rationalization of it.

But it must be remembered that, unlike Buddhism, the ancient autochthonous philosophies of China had no fixed creeds or articles of belief, and, like most literate Chinese of all periods of Chinese history, T'ao Ch'ien felt perfectly free to pick and choose among the ideas of the different philosophers, historians, and poets. Buddhism he utterly ignored, but from philosophical Taoism he took the idea of moral relativity—the Equality of Things and Opinions.[1] The following poem, entirely philosophical in content and not very valuable as poetry, illustrates this very clearly:

Of the hundred thousand facets
of human behaviour,

[1] Name of a chapter in the *Chuang Tzu*.

Who can ever know
    the wrong from the right?
When once right and wrong
    have fashioned one another,
Praise and blame go echoing
    like reverberating thunder.
In the Three Decadences[1]
    there was much of this—
The intelligent man
    will have no part of it,
But bids farewell
    to the fools of the vulgar herd,
And for his own part
    follows Huang and Ch'i.[2]

It was this bias in favour of moral relativity which explains his lack of moral indignation. An individualist through and through, he conceived that his whole duty to mankind was to be himself, to exercise and develop his own literary talents irrespective of what others might do or say. It was certainly reprehensibly selfish from the strictly Confucian point of view, but this was one of those cases where the results more than justified the "selfishness". Many of his contemporaries, like the old peasant who brought him a gift of wine (p. 67) and the well-meaning people who from time to time recommended him for official posts, may have sighed with dismay over such a waste of talent and ability as he seemed to exemplify. But, when all is said and done, posterity would not have had it otherwise. We would rather have the direct experience of knowing him as he was, through his poems, than perhaps to have read in some history that a certain T'ao Ch'ien had had

[1] Periods of decadence at the ends of the three earliest dynasties, Hsia, Shang, and Chou.

[2] Hsia Huang-kung and Ch'i Li-chi, two of four hermits called the Four Greybeards of Mt. Shang.

a brilliant career at court but had made enemies, had been slandered and died for his principles; or, that he had devoted his life to good works and lectured on Confucian ethics. As he saw it, his business was first, last, and foremost with himself: he was an artist, and the world has a way of justifying and recognizing such people in the end.

Substance, Shadow, and Spirit

Whether nobly born or humble, whether wise or simple, there is none who does not diligently seek to spare his own life, but in so doing men are greatly deluded. Therefore I have done my best to set forth the reasons for this in the form of an argument between Substance and Shadow which is finally resolved by Spirit who expounds Nature. May gentle‑men of an inquiring turn of mind take it to heart.

SUBSTANCE SPEAKS TO SHADOW

Heaven and Earth
    endure and do not perish;
Mountains and rivers
    do not change with time.
Grasses and trees partake
    in this constant principle,
Although the frost and dew
    cause them to wilt or flourish.
Of all things Man, they say,
    is most intelligent and wise,
And yet he alone
    is not like them in this.
Appearing by chance
    he comes into this world,
And suddenly is gone
    never to return.
How is one to feel
    the lack of such a one
When even friends and kinfolk
    scarcely think of him?
Only that the things
    he used in life are left—

Coming across them
　　may make us shed a tear.
I have no art
　　to soar and be transfigured;[1]
That it must be so
　　I cannot ever question.
I only beg that you
　　will agree with what I say
And when we can get wine
　　never perversely refuse it!

SHADOW REPLIES TO SUBSTANCE

I cannot tell you
　　how to preserve life,
And have always been inept
　　in the art of guarding it.[2]
Yet truly I desire
　　to roam on K'un and Hua[3]
But they are far away
　　and the road to them is lost.
Ever since I met you
　　and have been with you
I have known no other
　　sorrows and joys but yours.
Though I seemed to leave you
　　when you rested in the shade,
I really never left you
　　until the day was done.[4]
But this association
　　cannot last forever;
Mysteriously at last
　　we shall vanish in the darkness.
After our death—
　　that our name should also perish

At the mere thought of this
                the Five Passions seethe within me.
Should we not labour
                and strive with all our might
To do good in such a way
                that men will love us for it?
Wine, as they say,
                may dissipate our grief,
But how could it ever
                be compared to fame?

SPIRIT RESOLVES THE ARGUMENT

The Great Balance [5]
                has no personal power,
And its myriad veins
                interlace of themselves. [6]
That Man has his place
                among the Three Forces, [7]
This is certainly
                due to my presence with you.
And although I am
                different from you both,
At birth I am added
                and joined together with you.
Bound and committed
                to sharing good and evil
How can we avoid
                mutual exchange?
The Three Emperors [8]
                were the Primal Sages.
Now, after all,
                whither are they gone?
And though Grandfather P'eng [9]
                achieved longevity

Yet he too had to go
    when he still wished to stay.
Old and young
    all suffer the same death,
The wise and the foolish—
    uncounted multitudes.
Getting drunk daily
    one may perhaps forget
But is not wine a thing
    that shortens one's life?
And in doing good
    you may always find pleasure
But no one is obliged
    to give you praise for it.
Dwelling on such things
    wounds my very life.
The right thing to do
    is to leave things to Fate,
Let go and float along
    on the great flux of things,
Not overjoyed
    but also not afraid.
When it is time to go
    then we should simply go.
There is nothing after all
    that we can do about it.

---

[1] *According to popular Taoism which was gradually becoming institutionalized into a Church in T'ao Ch'ien's time, the adept could achieve these things by the practice of Taoist yoga (a system of breath control), an elaborate and strict sexual regimen and, above all, a strict diet with avoidance of grain and meat and reliance on vegetables, herbs, and drugs of various kinds. T'ao Ch'ien here shows himself to be rather sceptical of such claims.*

[2] *This refers specifically to Taoist yoga, sexual regimen, and diet which at the very least were supposed to confer longevity.*

³ *After long and successful practice of "the art of preserving life", culminating perhaps in the discovery of some elixir of immortality, the Taoist adept was supposed to become transfigured. His very body was transformed into some finer substance, and he soared away to certain realms of the immortals, where he lived in houses of gold and subsisted on air and dew. The K'un-lun mountains far in the west, Mt. Hua at the great bend of the Yellow River, and Mt. P'eng-lai floating in the midst of the Eastern ocean were believed to be such abodes.*

⁴ *The material soul (P'O), which unlike the spirit (variously called SHEN or HUN) remains with the body after death like a sort of lingering eddy of animal magnetism, was identified with the visible shadow. But it remained with the body, whether visible or not.*

⁵ *The TAO (Way) is the sum totality of all things, spirit and matter and the laws by which they operate, conceived of as one great monad. But though ultimately all is one, this monad expresses itself, operates, and ceaselessly creates through two apparently opposing forces, YIN (shade) and YANG (light). These terms are applied very widely to account for all sorts of dualities such as positive and negative, male and female, active and passive, etc. Neither one of these forces ever destroys or diminishes the other; the quantity and strength of each in the universe as a whole remain constant. The term TA CHÜN ("great scales", "great balance") expresses this truth, and so may almost be taken as an equivalent to Tao itself.*

⁶ *Within the Tao, YIN and YANG, spirit and matter, the passive and the active, are all inexhaustible, indestructible, and equal. All phenomena and effects, visible or invisible, are produced by their ceaseless motion and constant interplay. Although this view of the universe leaves no room for a personal God, or* deus ex machina, *it cannot be called atheistic or materialistic, but is closer to what we know as pantheism or monism.*

⁷ *The Three Cosmic Forces (SAN TS'AI) are Heaven, Earth, and Man. Chinese thought is by no means so un-anthropocentric as is commonly said.*

⁸ *Three mythical culture heroes of remote antiquity variously identified in early texts. Perhaps the most widely known trinities are Fu Hsi, Shen Neng, and Nü Kua; and Fu Hsi, Shen Neng, and Huang Ti.*

⁹ *The Chinese Methuselah, a very shadowy mythical figure who had no special cult, but was merely proverbial for longevity.*

Spending the Ninth Day[1] in Solitude

Though I was dwelling in solitude I still celebrated the Double Ninth Festival: Autumn chrysanthemums filled my garden and I had no wine at the time, so all I could do was to drink in the flowers of the Ninth Day and put my feelings into words.

> Our lives are short
>   and our ambitions many:
> That is why people
>   desire longevity.
> So when the ninth day
>   of the ninth month
> Following the Zodiac
>   comes round in its turn
> People everywhere
>   love to celebrate it.
> The dews are frozen
>   and the signs of Heaven bright,
> Not a shadow remains
>   of the swallows that have gone,
> But the air resounds
>   with the cries of wild geese coming.
> And while one can with wine
>   exorcize all sorrows
> Chrysanthemums know how
>   to restrain declining years.
> How is it with me
>   the thatch-cottage scholar,

Vainly watching how
    my time and fate decline?
While my dusty cup
    shames the empty wine-jar,[2]
These cold-weather flowers
    bloom of themselves alone.
I pull close my lapels
    and sing to myself at leisure,
Which somehow distantly
    awakens deep emotions.
Even in retirement
    I do have many pleasures,
Even in my lassitude
    I still get things accomplished.

[1] *The ninth day of the ninth month was a popular holiday when people would climb hills for picnics, with a view of obtaining longevity, in commemoration of the escape of Huan Ching from a massacre of which he had been forewarned by the magician Fei Chang-fang.*

[2] *It would never be dusty if there were wine in the jar.*

FIVE POEMS
ON RETURNING TO DWELL IN
THE COUNTRY

I

In youth I had nothing
    that matched the vulgar tone,
For my nature always
    loved the hills and mountains.
Inadvertently I fell
    Into the Dusty Net,[1]
Once having gone
    it was more than thirteen years.[2]
The tame bird
    longs for his old forest—
The fish in the house-pond
    thinks of his ancient pool.
I too will break the soil
    at the edge of the Southern moor,
I will guard simplicity
    and return to my fields and garden.
My land and house—
    a little more than ten acres,
In the thatched cottage—
    only eight or nine rooms.
Elms and willows
    shade the back verandah,
Peach and plum trees
    in rows before the hall.

Hazy and dimly seen
    a village in the distance,
Close in the foreground
    the smoke of neighbours' houses.
A dog barks
    amidst the deep lanes,
A cock is crowing
    atop a mulberry tree.
No dust and confusion
    within my doors and courtyard;
In the empty rooms,
    more than sufficient leisure.
Too long I was held
    within the barred cage.
Now I am able
    to return again to Nature.

[1] *i.e. "the World".*

[2] *The various editions all have "thirty years", but as the commentators point out, T'ao Ch'ien's first official post, which he assumed in A.D. 392, was Libationer of his District, and he left his last post of Governor of the District of P'eng-tse in A.D. 406. (See p. 24.)*

II

Here in the Country
    I have little to do with people,
In my poor lane
    no noise of wheel and harness.
White sunlight
    bathes the rustic gate,
The empty rooms
    cut off dusty thoughts.
At times I find myself
    again among my neighbours,
Parting the high grass
    we walk about together.
Meeting each other
    we do not talk at random,
But only speak of how
    the hemp and mulberry grow.
Hemp and mulberry
    keep growing day by day
And every day I clear
    the land a little more.
My constant fear
    is of the frost and hail
Which could reduce my crops
    to a mass of tangled grasses.

III

I planted beans beneath the southern hill,
While the grass is thick the bean shoots still are sparse.
Rising at dawn I pull up weeds and tares,
Shouldering my hoe I carry home the moon.[1]
The path is narrow, the grass and bushes high—
The evening dew has thoroughly drenched my clothes.
That my clothes are wet I do not mind at all:
It only makes me wish not to avoid what comes.[2]

[1] *A figurative expression which appears to mean that, looking back over his shoulder, the poet sees the moon as though it were a bundle suspended from the handle of his hoe. This line is much admired by Chinese critics.*

[2] *Literally: "to practice non-avoidance" or "non-contrariety", that is to say, to act in conformity with the Tao. Every kind of work brings with it its own discomforts and frustrations, and he must learn to accept the bad with the good.*

IV

Long I have loved to stroll among the hills and marshes,
And take my pleasure roaming the woods and fields.
Now I hold hands with a train of nieces and nephews,
Parting the hazel growth we tread the untilled wastes—
Wandering to and fro amidst the hills and mounds
Everywhere around us are dwellings of ancient men.
Here are vestiges of their wells and hearthstones,
There the rotted stumps of bamboo and mulberry groves.
I stop and ask a faggot-gatherer:[1]
"These men—what has become of them?"
The faggot-gatherer turns to me and says:
"Once they were dead that was the end of them."
In the same world men lead different lives;
Some at the court, some in the market-place.
Indeed I know these are no empty words:
The life of man is like a shadow-play
Which must in the end return to nothingness.

[1] *In Chinese poetry the faggot-gatherer and the fisherman are types of the
rustic philosopher. Perhaps the man might have been some sort of hermit. There
are endless stories telling how this or that emperor goes out hunting and meets
such a man and is so struck with his wisdom that he takes him back to court
and gives him high office, or in other cases the man refuses to go.*

V

In grief and disappointment I return with my staff alone,[1]
Over the rugged path I thread its hazeled windings.
A mountain stream runs clear and shallow,
Coming upon it I wade and wash my feet.[2]
Arriving home I filter my newly heated wine
And killing chickens invite in all my neighbours.
The sun goes down—it is dark within the hall,
And thornwood faggots take the place of candles.
When such joys come the bitter night is short
And so it goes until the day dawns in the east.

[1] *Reflecting with pain on the words of the faggot-gatherer he feels suddenly old, and as he goes the path seems steep and difficult.*

[2] *This, presumably, makes him feel better, and he conceives the idea of inviting his neighbours in for feasting and talking.*

On Several Men Having a Picnic

Beneath the Cedars of the Grave-mounds of the Chou Family[1]

Indeed today
    the heaven's breath is fine
And blows so pure
    as to sound like ringing lutes.
Moved at the sight
    of those men beneath the cedars
How could it fail
    to rejoice together with them!
With clear singing
    we pour forth the new tones,
And the green wine
    opens its fragrant face—
True, we do not know
    what may come tomorrow
But our inmost thoughts
    we have utterly laid bare.

[1] *This family and T'ao Ch'ien's had intermarried for generations. The grave-mound was probably not far from his home.*

A Resentful Poem in the Ch'u Mode[1]

The Way of Heaven is recondite and far
And ghosts and spirits vague and indistinct.
Since my hair was bound [2] I have tried to do my best—
And laboured hard for more than fifty years.
Even as a lad I met the world's rebuffs
And lost the mate of my first marriage.[3]
Lowering flames repeatedly burned my house
And grubs and weevils had their will of my fields.
The wind and rain came slashing and pouring down
So that the harvests never filled the markets—
On summer days I always hugged my hunger.
On frosty nights I could not sleep for cold.
When evening came I could only think of cockcrow
When the day dawned I could only long for sunset.
It was all in *me*, how could I blame Heaven?
To depart from sorrow one must suffer in the present.
Alas, alas fame beyond death
To me is as a floating cloud.
With high-hearted grief I sadly sing alone.
Chung Ch'i who knew the notes[4] was intelligent indeed.

[1] *Songs of sorrow and resentment were so called.*

[2] *When boys reached the age of twenty their hair was bound, which formed part of the ceremony of initiation to manhood.*

[3] *At twenty T'ao Ch'ien lost his first wife and later married into the Ti clan.*

[4] *T'ao Ch'ien here expresses a longing for such a friend as Chung Tzu-ch'i, whose mind was so perfectly attuned to that of his friend Po-ya (see note 2 on p. 81) that when the latter played the lute while thinking of high mountains and flowing waters, Chung knew it at once. When Chung Tzu-ch'i died, Po-ya tore the strings from his lute and broke it, saying that there was now no one to whom he could play.*

On Moving House

I

That I had long desired
    to dwell in the Southern village
Was not because the house
    had been declared auspicious—
Only that I had heard
    there were many plain-minded people
With whom it were a joy
    to count the mornings and evenings.
I cherished the plan
    for quite a number of years,
But today at last
    I am really moving house.
My modest dwelling
    why need it be large?
Just so there is room
    for my bed and mats.
Neighbours and friends
    will come from time to time,
And with brave words
    we will talk of things of old.
Joyfully we will praise
    rare poetry together,
And settle doubtful meanings
    by mutual discussion.

II

In the Spring and Autumn
    are many fine days
When I climb the heights
    to compose new verses.
Passing the doors of friends
    we call to one another
Or when there is wine
    we drink a cup together.
When from his husbandry
    each one returns alone
Suddenly in his leisure
    one will think of the other.
Thinking of his friend
    he will don his coat and go,
And laugh and talk with him
    without ever growing weary.
Just when this mood
    has reached its highest pitch
That is no time
    to be in haste to go.
Clothing and food
    will surely be arranged for—
Hard work with the plough
    never will deceive us.

Living in retirement I had few pleasures, and moreover the autumn nights were already growing longer. I happened to have some wine from a famous place, and this I drank every evening. I would finish it alone sitting self-contentedly, and suddenly would find myself drunk again. After I was drunk, I would quickly dash off a few verses to amuse myself. After a while the paper and ink made quite a pile, though the pieces had no logical sequence, so I merely asked a friend to write them out for me for a happy laugh.

I

Fortune and misfortune
    have no fixed abode;
This one and the other
    are given us in turn.
Shao P'ing working
    in his field of melons
Was much as he had been
    when Lord of Tung-ling.[1]
Cold and hot seasons
    follow one another,
And the way of man
    will always be like this.

The intelligent man
    sees that it must be so.
Having gone so far
    he will not doubt again,
But from that moment
    every day and evening
He will be happy
    holding a cup of wine.

[1] *Shao P'ing was Marquis of Tung-ling when the Han overthrew the Ch'in dynasty in 206 B.C. Losing all his rank, he was reduced to growing melons on land east of the Ch'ang-an city wall. They were of exceptionally fine quality and became famous as "Tung-ling melons".*

II

Men say that doing good has its sure reward,
Yet Po-i and Shu-ch'i died on the Western Hill.[1]
If good comes not from good nor evil out of evil
Why go to all the trouble of vainly saying so?
Master Jung[2] roamed at ninety with a rope for girdle,
And hunger and cold are cruel at that age.
Had he not known how to rise above poverty and want,
Who would speak of him after a thousand years?

[1] *Legendary brothers who remained true to the corrupt and decadent Shang dynasty when it fell (1122 B.C.), and preferred to live on thorn-ferns on Mt. Shou till they starved to death rather than eat the grain of the new Chou dynasty.*

[2] *A reference to the story of Jung Ch'i-ch'i which is as follows: When Confucius was travelling on T'ai-shan he saw Jung Ch'i-ch'i playing his lute and singing, clad in a deerskin with a rope for his girdle, and asked him why he was so happy. Jung replied: "My joys are very many! Of all the myriad things that Heaven has produced, man is the noblest, and I am a man. This is my first joy. Of male and female, the male is more honourable and I am a male. This is my second joy. And of men that are born some die in swaddling clothes without ever seeing the sun or moon, but I have passed my ninetieth year. This is my third joy. Poverty is the usual lot of the gentleman; death is the end of all men. If I meet my end sharing the common lot, what is there sad in this?" "Excellently said," said Confucius, "Here is a man who has found freedom!"*

III

The Tao has been lost
    nigh on a thousand years
And people everywhere
    are misers of their feelings.
Though they have wine
    they do not dare to drink it,
And think of nothing save
    keeping their reputation.
All the things that make us
    care about our lives—
They are surely compassed
    within a single lifetime.
And how much can that life
    amount to after all—
Swift as the surprise
    of pouring lightning,
Fixed and circumscribed
    within a hundred years—
Hemmed and bound to this
    what can we hope to do?

IV

I built my house near where others dwell,
And yet there is no clamour of carriages and horses.
You ask of me "How can this be so?"
"When the heart is far the place of itself is distant."
I pluck chrysanthemums under the eastern hedge,
And gaze afar towards the southern mountains.
The mountain air is fine at evening of the day
And flying birds return together homewards.
Within these things there is a hint of Truth,
But when I start to tell it, I cannot find the words.

V

In the clear dawn
    I hear a knocking at my gate
And skirt on wrong way round
    go to open it myself.
I ask the visitor
    "Pray, sir, who may you be?"
It is an old peasant
    who had a kindly thought,
And has come from far away
    bearing a jug of wine,
Because he thinks I am
    at variance with the times.
"Sitting in patched clothes
    under a thatched roof—
This will never help you
    to get on in the world!
All the world together
    praises that alone,
So I wish, sir, that you too
    would float with the muddy stream."
"Old man, I am deeply
    grateful for your words,
But your advice does not accord
    with my inborn nature.
Even if I could learn
    to follow the curb and reins,
To go against one's nature
    is always a mistake.
Let us just be happy
    and drink this wine together—
I fear my chariot
    can never be turned back."

VI

Once I had a guest
    who lived together with me,
And yet our tastes
    were very far apart.
For the one was always
    getting drunk alone,
While the other was sober
    the whole year round.
The drunk and the sober
    still laughed at one another,
And neither would accept
    a word the other said.
Aghast and astonished
    at how different we were,
We grew proud and stubborn
    each in his own conceit.
But this is my advice
    to the drunken traveller,
"When the sun goes down
    let him take his lamp in hand."[1]

[1] *This is an allusion to one of the famous NINETEEN OLD POEMS which had served as models for generations of poets writing in the five-word metre. It has been so beautifully translated by Arthur Waley as to constitute a little classic of English poetry, and I give his translation of it here in full, since T'ao Ch'ien frequently quotes from the original in the poems which follow:*

"The years of a lifetime do not reach a hundred,
Yet they contain a thousand years' sorrow.
When days are short and the dull nights long,
Why not take a lamp and wander forth?
If you want to be happy you must do it now,
There is no waiting till an after-time.
The fool who's loath to spend the wealth he's got
Becomes the laughing-stock of after ages.
It is true that Master Wang became immortal,
But how can we hope to share his lot?"

(170 CHINESE POEMS, *translated by Arthur Waley.)**

* *Reprinted by permission of Alfred A. Knopf, Inc., New York* *(Copyright 1919, 1941), and Constable and Company Ltd., London.*

On Stopping Wine

Dwelling, I stopped
    close to the city wall.
And my wanderings
    stopped with staying home.
Sitting, I stop
    under the lofty shade,
Walking, I stop
    within my wattled gate.
For me, good eating
    stops with my garden mallows.
And for me, great joy
    stopped with childhood.
Since then from day to day
    I have never stopped wine,
For if I stopped it
    my feelings knew no pleasure.
Stopping at evening
    I could not get to sleep,
Stopping at dawn
    I could not even rise.
Yet from day to day
    I have wished to stop.
When all my hopes and plans
    stopped, and did not thrive.
All that I knew
    was that stopping was a hardship,
And never could believe
    stopping could profit me.
At last having understood
    that it were well to stop,

This very morning
    I have really stopped,
And now, henceforward,
    from this stopping on,
I shall be stopping
    on the shores of Fairyland.
My clear visage
    will stop the morning-after face
And may this never stop
    for a hundred thousand years!

I

The bright sun sinks
    beyond the western ridge,
The white moon rises
    behind the eastern range.
Afar, afar
    a myriad miles it flashes,
Immeasurably vast
    its light amidst the sky.
A wind comes
    and enters the bedroom door,
So in the night
    pillow and mat are cold.
The air seems different—
    I awake to the season's change.
I cannot go to sleep
    and know the night's eternity,
I wish to speak
    but there is no friend to talk to.
Raising my cup
    I challenge my lonely shadow.
The days and months
    fling us aside and pass;
We have high purposes
    but cannot realize them.
Thinking of this
    I have grief and pain at heart,
And all night long
    can find no quietness.

II

It is hard to dwell long in prosperity;
Rise and decline cannot be reckoned on.
What were formerly lotus buds in May,
Now in the autumn are but withered seed-pods.
A heavy frost stiffens the prairie grasses—
They wilt despondently and do not quickly die.
The sun and moon come ever circling back.
Once *we* depart we do not shine again.
I ponder deeply on times long past and gone
Though to remember them tears my very entrails.

III

The valiant warrior
    dreams of the Four Seas.
All I desire
    is not to know old age,
To have my family
    together in one place,
Sons and grandsons
    cherishing one another,
With cup and strings
    to entertain the morning sun,
The wine in my wine jars
    never to run dry,
With loosened girdle
    exhaust my cup of pleasure
To get up late and always
    quickly go to sleep—
How would it be for all
    the gentry of the world
To take to their hearts
    charcoal and ice alike?[1]
Within a hundred years
    all go home to their grave-mounds.
Remembering that,
    it is vain to make distinctions.[2]

---

[1] *In the biography of Fu I of the Later Han dynasty the following sentence occurs: "The heterodox (non-Confucians) and the orthodox should not share the (same) country any more than one can put ice and charcoal in the same vessel."*

[2] *i.e. make distinctions among people on the basis of their opinions and beliefs. This is a plea for philosophic and religious tolerance.*

IV

I remember as a boy and later in my prime
Even without diversions I was glad and self-contained.
My fierce ambitions transcended the Four Seas
With trembling wings I dreamed of distant soarings.
But imperceptibly the years and months slipped by,
And that state of mind little by little left me.
Now, when pleasures come I no longer can enjoy them.
Cares and anxieties increase on every hand.
My strength of spirit has gradually waned
And my quick perceptions slacken from day to day.
But the hollow boat which knows no tarrying,
Carries me along so that I cannot stay
Ahead of me I have a little way to go
Though I do not know where I shall spend the night—
The men of old grudged an inch of shadow.[1]
Thinking of this fills my heart with fear.

---

[1] *The north side of a hill, hence shade. Here, of course, the reference is to a sundial. In the ancient philosophical work known as HUAI-NAN-TZU it is said that "the Sage does not value a piece of jade a foot in diameter, but puts a higher value on every inch of shade".*

V

Formerly when I heard
    the precepts of my elders,
I would stop my ears
    and never wished to listen.
But (I cannot help it)
    after these fifty years—
Suddenly I myself
    am saying the same things.
And as for seeking
    the pleasures of my prime
Not by a single hair
    do I desire them now.
On and on I go
    rolling ever faster,
How shall I ever
    meet this life again?
Often I made merry
    till I lost my household—
At last to this place
    the years and months have brought me.
Though I have children
    I never kept my money,
What was the use of saving
    for times beyond my death?[1]

[1] *Quis scit an adiciant hodiernae crastina summae*
    Tempora di superi?
Cuncta manus avidas fugient heredis, amico
    Quae dederis animo.

                            Horace, Lib. IV, VII.

"*Who knows whether the Gods on high will add any tomorrows to today's score? But all those things which you enjoy [now] will escape the greedy hands of your heir.*"

VI

The days and months do not wish to tarry,
The four seasons urge each other on.
A cold wind sweeps the withered branches,
And fallen leaves cover the long road.
My youthful vigour fails as the years revolve
And my black locks are already turning white.
When once the white signpost is raised above man's head
The road before him begins to seem narrow.
My home is only a hostel by the wayside,
And I a traveller who must soon depart.
On and on I travel—whither am I going?
On the Southern Mountain there is my ancient home.[1]

[1] *Presumably his family's burial-ground.*

VII

I have never wished
    a substitute for ploughing[1]
And all my work has been
    among the fields and orchards.
I have never yet
    utterly failed my family
Even though cold and hungry
    they always had bran and gruel.
How can I expect
    more than to fill my belly?
All I desire
    is enough grain to eat,
Blankets enough
    to keep out winter's cold—
Linen and grasscloth
    suitable for summer.
If after honest toil
    one cannot get these things,
Indeed it is sad
    and also pitiable.
Other people seem
    to have everything they want;
Only my clumsy self
    has not found the formula.
What is there now
    that I can do about it?
Just pour myself a cup
    and drink it joyfully.

[1] *i.e. "artificial" activities such as trade or public service as an official.*

78

I

Lofty, lofty, the hundred-foot tower,
Clear and distinct the view on the Four Wastes.[1]
In the evening it is the mansion of homing clouds
In the morning it becomes a hall for flying birds.
The mountains and rivers overwhelm the eye,
The level plain stretches vague and lonely.
From ancient times great and famous men
With noble courage fought over all this ground.
Now one morning after a hundred years
They are met together back at the Northern Mounds.
There the pines and cedars all have been cut down,
And the lofty mounds stand naked and alone.
No soul-tablets stand upon the crumbling altars,
The souls that were in them where are they roaming
    now?
Honour and glory indeed are to be prized
And yet at the same time are also pitiable!

[1] *Wild and unknown regions beyond the confines of the world of the ancient Chinese, but here of course it simply means the country round about in all four directions.*

II

The sun has set
    no clouds are in the sky
And the spring wind
    fans us faintly, gently.
And gentle friends
    loving this clear night
Have drunk and sung with me
    all the way till dawn.
When the songs were ended
    long I sighed and wept.
And many others there
    felt the same emotion.
Brilliantly white
    the moon amidst the clouds,
Flamingly clear
    the flowers amidst the leaves.
We should enjoy ourselves
    once without restraint,
For, before long,
    what will become of us?

III

When I was young I was strong and keen,
Stroking my sword I wandered the world alone.
And who can say I did not wander far—
From distant Chang-i all the way to Yu-chou![1]
Starving, I ate the thorn-fern of Mount Shou-yang.
Thirsting, I drank the waters of Yi River.
Coming to a place where no men were to be seen,
All that I saw were venerable grave-mounds.
By the side of the road there were two lofty tombs—
The resting-places of Chuang Chou and Po-ya.[2]
Men such as they will scarcely be found again
With all my travelling, what was *I* attempting!

[1] *Chang-i was a district on the far western border near Tun-huang. Yu-chou was an ancient name for north-eastern China.*

[2] *Chuang Chou, better known as Chuang Tzu, was the author or "sheltering worthy" of the ancient Taoist text known as the CHUANG TZU, which contains some of the greatest prose in the whole of Chinese literature. For Po-ya, see note 4 on p. 59.*

A Picnic by the Hsieh River

On the fifth day of the first month of the year *hsin ch'ou* (A.D. 401),[1] the weather being clear and mild and the scene tranquilly beautiful, I went on an excursion to Hsieh River with a few of my neighbours. Looking down over a long stretch of the river we could see the site of the walled city of Ts'eng[2] in the distance. As the evening came on we caught the flashing scales of bream and trout leaping from the water, and seagulls circled back and forth on the mild air.

The fame of the sites on the southern foothills of Mt. Lu is indeed ancient—it were a pity indeed not to celebrate them anew. There is the site of Ts'eng with nothing round about it, standing isolated on the river-bank. The sight of it awakened far-off memories of the fame of Mt. Ling.[3]

I felt that it was not enough simply to gaze at it enraptured, so on a sudden impulse I composed a poem in which I sorrowed over the way in which our days and months slip by, and grieved over how our years will not tarry. Each of us then noted his age and birthplace to form a record of the occasion.

> The fifth day of the New Year
>   was here before we knew it,
> And we suddenly felt
>   our lives were fading fast.
> Thinking of this
>   our hearts were moved within us,
> So while we yet have time
>   we have come to view this spot.
> The air is mild
>   and the heavens cloudless,

We spread our mats in order
    overlooking the far stream.
Speckled bream
    leapt in the slow eddies—
And crying gulls
    soared in the lonely vale.
We let our eyes wander
    at will over distant lowlands
And gazed with heart-felt longing
    at the far-off hill of Ts'eng.
True, it is not as high
    as the Nine-Storeyed Mountain,[4]
But no other hill commands
    such loving admiration.
Raising the ewer
    I call to my companions,
Draining our cups
    we pledge and pledge again.
After all who knows
    in the time to come
We may not ever
    meet like this again.
Midway in our cups
    we give rein to far-off feelings
And utterly forget
    the "thousand years of sorrow".[5]
Let us just enjoy
    this day to the utmost
And let our tomorrows
    take care of themselves.

¹ *Thus, in T'ao Ch'ien's thirty-seventh year.*

² *In T'ao Ch'ien's time a Buddhist temple called Lo-hsing-ssu (Temple of the Falling Star) stood upon the site.*

³ *There are several mountains called Ling-shan in China, but here the reference must be to Ling-chiu-shan, the Vulture Peak (in Sanskrit Grdhra-kuta) in India where the Buddha Sakya-muni preached the Law.*

⁴ *A fabulous place in the K'un-lun Mountains, mentioned in the HUAI-NAN-TZU.*

⁵ *See note 1 on pp. 68 and 69.*

In Answer to a Poem by Commander P'ang

After you had deigned to pay me several visits I could not have discontinued the relationship [1] even had I wished to—and since that time we have seen each other like close neighbours through the winter and the spring, and entertained one another with such easy informality that in no time we became close friends. There is a common phrase, "Already old friends after several meetings", but how greatly does our mutual feeling surpass what that implies. No matter whether a personal relationship goes well or ill, the time always comes to say good-bye—the thing that Yang Chu sighed at [2]—and this must be our constant sorrow.

I have been cherishing an illness for so many years that I can never really produce literature. Nevertheless, though from the beginning I was never prolific, I keep on trying, old and ill as I am. Thus, it suddenly occurred to me to use the "coming and going of friends" spoken of in the *Rites of Chou* as material for a poem on friends thinking of one another after parting.

> Mutual acquaintance—
> > why need it be old?
> "Meeting on the road" [3]
> > has been spoken of before.
> I have a friend
> > who understands my taste,
> Ever and again
> > he reviews my woods and gardens.
> In our conversations
> > no hint of vulgar themes—
> What we discuss
> > are the writings of the Sages.

Sometimes we have
        several pots of wine
Which we drink at leisure
        in natural contentment.
Indeed, I am
        a far-hidden hermit,
With what is east or west
        I have no more connexions.
When things are new
        if but the man be "old",[4]
With a tender brush-tip
        much can be expressed—
Emotions penetrate
        beyond ten thousand miles,
While the bodily form
        is held by hills and streams.
Meanwhile be sparing
        of your body's substance
Against the year
        when you will come again!

[1] *T'ao Ch'ien ordinarily had as little to do with people as possible.*

[2] *Yang Chu (c. 500 B.C.) was a philosopher contemporary with Mo Tzu (the advocate of universal love), who not only derided and opposed the latter's views, but also Confucian ethics which were based primarily on filial piety and family relationships; he insisted that death was the only reality, and that each individual should strive only to realize his own potentialities, disregarding all other considerations.*

[3] *Literally, "tilting the chariot tops, or covers". The top of the typical ancient Chinese chariot was a sort of parasol or umbrella fixed to a mast in the centre of the car. For reasons not clear the term means two chariots meeting and stopping abreast of one another on a road so that their occupants might converse while standing in them. (Ref. Confucius and Ch'eng-tzu.)*

[4] *i.e. when there is some news to tell, one can write it to a friend, whether he be old in the sense that one has known him a long time, or "old" in the sense that he was congenial at first meeting, and quickly became intimate.*

Written on the First Day
of the Fifth Month

Harmonizing with a Poem by the Registrar Tai

The empty boat [1]
    drifts on and on at will
Till it returns at last
    into infinity.
After Spring came
    I had hardly looked around
When suddenly it was
    the middle of the year.
By the southern windows
    no trace of tiresome things,
And the northern woods
    are dense and flowering.
The deep abyss of Heaven
    sends the season's rain.
And the morning's colour
    heralds the south wind.
Once come into this world
    there is none but must depart,
But that is not the end
    of the meaning of our lives.
To dwell in what is constant
    and so await the end,
Though one's only pillow
    should be his bended arm [2]
That will not destroy
    his inner quietness.

Becoming an Immortal
    is a steep and dangerous road
But to set one's own ideals
    is a broad and level highway.
If we are lofty
    in our everyday pursuits
What would be the use
    of climbing Hua or Sung.[3]

---

[1] *Human life is compared to a boat drifting on the stream of time; cf. p. 75, l. 11.*

[2] *"The Master said, He who seeks only coarse food to eat, water to drink and a bent arm for pillow, will without looking for it find happiness to boot."*

                                    (Waley, ANALECTS, VII, 15.)

[3] *Hua-shan and Sung-shan are two of the Five Sacred Mountains of ancient China, both also fabled abodes of Taoist Immortals and adepts.*

Putting the Blame on His Sons

White hair covers my temples—
My flesh is no longer firm,
And though I have five sons
Not one cares for brush and paper.
Ah-shu is sixteen years of age;
For laziness he surely has no equal.
Ah-hsüan tries his best to learn
But does not really love the arts.
Yung and Tuan at thirteen years
Can hardly distinguish six from seven;
T'ung-tzu with nine years behind him
Does nothing but hunt for pears and chestnuts.
If such was Heaven's decree
In spite of all that I could do,
Bring on, bring on
The Thing Within the Cup.

Written after Meeting a Friend

This poem is based on a story given in the BOOK OF RITES. Once when there was a great famine in the state of C'hi, a certain Ch'in Ao set up a soup kitchen by the roadside in order to feed the starv-ing, to which they came in droves. One hungry man came up covering his face with his sleeve to hide his shame, while Ch'in Ao was shouting "Ah, come on and eat!" Hearing this rough and unrefined invitation to eat, this man uncovered his face, raised his eyes to look at Ch'in Ao, and said, "I simply cannot eat when invited to do so with words like 'come and get it'." He turned away, refused to eat, and soon starved to death. T'ao Ch'ien takes strong exception to this exaggerated reaction, and points out that Ch'in Ao's good intention had been made clear by his having provided the food and that to expect ceremonial behaviour of him in addition was quite out of place. The man who covered his face may have been well-to-do and nobly born, and so have felt his starved condition as an intense humiliation, but he should have remembered how even Confucius, greatest of sages was once starved and menaced in the course of a journey, and how, on being asked by one of his disciples whether such things should befall a gentleman, he had replied, "Assuredly a gentleman is some-times in adversity." The poem with T'ao's prose preface follows:

"Already the old grain is gone and the new grain has not yet come up."[1] I have lived rather a long time on the land and have known famine in my day, and though that was long ago I am even now worried about it again. Since I cannot yet be sure of a successful harvest, what we have to depend on from morning to evening will barely suffice for our daily needs, but only within the last ten days have I begun to think that we may yet suffer want. Whenever the year begins to turn towards its evening, this is for ever my sorrowful concern, but if I do not now set it forth, how will posterity hear about it?

In childhood I knew
        poverty in my home,
Now Old Age has come
        I still am always hungry.
Pulse and wheat
        are all that I aspire to—
How should I dare to long
        for what is sweet or rich?
My hunger is scarcely less
        than the "nine meal"[2] fast
And in the summer heat
        I loathe my winter clothes.
Now that the year
        is drawing towards its evening,
How great is my suffering,
        bitterness and sorrow.
I have always liked the mind
        of the man who gave the gruel,
And deeply loathed the pride
        of him who hid behind his sleeve.
When the giver shouted,
        "Ah, come on and eat!"
What was there in that
        to be offended at,
And perish to no purpose
        leaving an empty name?
Such an excess as that
        but mocked the giver's purpose;

"Even the Sage must suffer"[3]
    ought to have been his refuge.
After all, there comes an end
    even to being hungry,
And from Antiquity
    there is much that we can learn.

[1] *A quotation from the ANALECTS of Confucius used as a sort of scriptural text.*

[2] *When Tzu Ssu, one of Confucius' disciples, was in the state of Wei, he had only nine meals during thirty days.*

[3] *See my remarks on p. 90, and note 1 on p. 127.*

Harmonizing with a Poem by Liu Ch'ai-sang

Long I have felt the call of the hills and marshes
What could be the reason for my hesitation!
First of all I'd see my old friends and kinsmen
And never have it said that I proudly dwelt apart.
On an auspicious day a strange mood came upon me,
And taking up my staff I returned to the Western Lodge.
On the weed-grown road no one was going home—
And from time to time I passed abandoned home-sites.
I will set to work and prepare new thatching,
And the fallow acres must be tilled again.
Now the East Wind is turning chill and cheerless
Last Spring's unstrained wine will dispel my hungry
                                        tiredness—
Just as a young girl, though no literary friend,[1]
Is better than no one to assuage my feelings.
While we are busy with the world's affairs,
The years and months chase each other on—
Ploughing and weaving will satisfy our needs—
Beyond these things what should we require?
On and on we go—after a hundred years
Body and name alike will be hidden and forgotten.

---

[1] *I am not quite sure, but I think he means that whereas it would have been better to have vintage wine and first-class literary men to talk to, there in his own countryside (on the occasion of writing this poem at least) he has only the wine which he himself brewed last spring, and a young girl to keep him company. The "young girl" could have been a daughter, a mistress, a concubine —there is no way of knowing. See Appendix I.*

In Reply to a Poem by Liu Ch'ai-sang

Dwelling in poverty
    I have few human contacts
And at times forget
    the turning of the seasons.
In the empty court
    are many fallen leaves—
With pain at my heart
    I know that Fall has come.
New sunflowers
    shade the north window,
Fine ripe grain
    enriches the southern acres.
If I do not take
    this chance to be happy
How do I know that I
    shall see another harvest?
Calling the children to me
    I take them by the hand
On this fine day
    let us climb and roam afar.

Harmonizing with a Poem by the Registrar Kuo

I

Shady, shady, the woods before the hall,
In the midst of summer treasuring pure shadow.
A gentle wind comes from time to time
And eddying about blows open my lapels.
Parting from company I go and rest at leisure,
Or getting up again I play with books and lute.
Vegetables from my garden provide nourishment to spare,
Of grain from last year's harvest there is still enough in store.
Really I have managed as well as I could do,
To have more than I needed was never my desire.
Husking my millet I brew exquisite wine,
When the wine is ready I dip it out myself.
The young children play beside my seat,
Learning to talk they do not yet form words.
With all these things I have regained happiness
And with their help forget the flowered hairpin.[1]
Afar, afar, I gaze at the white clouds,
And think of olden days with Oh, how deep a longing.

II

It was mild and fresh through the three months of Spring,
Clear and cool is the white autumn season
When frozen dews give out no floating vapours,
The heavens are high and the awesome view is clear.
From the high ranges soar up lofty peaks—
Seen from afar incomparably rare.

Fragrant chrysanthemums are bright among the trees
Where the green pines crown the serried rocks.
Remembering how these chaste and lovely forms
Loftily became heroes beneath the frosts,
With cup to lip I think of you lovely ones—
For a thousand years I will cherish your parting words.
Carefully examining the plain stuff of life
I find I cannot ever fully reveal it.
Therefore let me be joyful and serene
And in this way live out all my days.

<hr />

[1] *An ornate hairpin used to fasten an official's cap of office in place.*

Seeing Off a Guest at Captain Wang's Headquarters

The autumn days
    are terrible and keen,
And the hundred herbs
    will soon all be withered.
Now in the season
    when we tread the frost
I climb on high
    to see you off again.
Cold air
    obscures the hills and lowlands
So that the floating clouds
    have no place to rest.
Unthinkably far
    the islets of the ocean,
And the wind and waves
    are often contrary.
As evening comes on
    we enjoy the farewell banquet
Though our parting words
    must at last be sad,
When the birds of dawn
    return to roost at evening
And the setting sun
    gathers his last rays in.
Going and staying—
    to each a different road,
And I grieve how long before
    your chariot returns.

My eyes will follow
  your boat into the distance,
And my emotions fade
  with the Ten-thousand Changes.[1]

On Reading the Classic of the Hills and Seas

By the early summer
 grasses and trees have grown
And around my roof
 the spaced trees join branches.
The flocks of birds
 are glad to have their refuge,
I no less than they
 love my little house.
Ploughing is done
 and also I have sown—
The time has come
 to return and read my books.
The narrow lane—
 deep ruts on either side—
Rather deters
 the carriages of friends!
Contentedly I sit
 and pour the new spring wine,
Or go out to pluck
 vegetables in my garden.
A gentle shower
 approaches from the east
And a pleasant wind
 comes along with it.
I read at length
 the story of King Mu,[1]
And let my gaze wander
 over pictures of hills and seas.[2]

Thus with a glance I reach
    the ends of the Universe—
If this is not a pleasure
    where could I ever find one?

[1] *Of the Chou dynasty, regn. 1001–946 B.C. A romantic account of his adventures in the West, where it is related that he reached the K'un-lun Mountains and visited the legendary Hsi Wang Mu or Queen Mother of the West, is extant. It is said to have been discovered in an early Chou tomb, and thus to be a very early work, but its authenticity is in doubt.*

[2] *In T'ao Ch'ien's time books were in scroll form and were very often profusely illustrated. Since the book was a scroll, he could see as much of it at a time as he pleased.*

THREE SONGS
WRITTEN IN IMITATION
OF ANCIENT BEARERS' SONGS[1]

I

Where there is life
    there also must be death—
Yet Fate did not compel him
    to an untimely end.[2]
Yesterday evening
    he was a man among us
At dawn today he was
    on the Roster of the Ghosts.
His spirit, scattered—
    whither has it gone
While the withered frame
    dwells in the empty wood?
A pretty little boy
    cries as he seeks his father
And our kindly neighbours
    weep as they comfort us.
Success or failure
    he will not know again,
Questions of right or wrong
    mean nothing to him now.
In a thousand autumns—
    after ten thousand years,

[1] cf. Waley, 170 CHINESE POEMS.
[2] i.e. the deceased had a fairly long and happy life.

Who will know whether
    he had glory or disgrace?
The only pity is
    while he was in the world
Of drinking wine
    he never got enough.

II

There were often times
    when we had no wine to drink,
However, this morning
    we fill the empty beakers.
Over the new spring wine
    floating midges hover—
When will we ever
    taste its like again?
Tables with funeral meats
    stand piled high before us,
Old friends and relatives
    come and weep beside us.
We try to speak
    but cannot utter words,
We try to see
    but our eyes are dim.
Once he used to sleep
    within the lofty hall,
Now he will spend the night
    out on the lonely moor.
Leaving the city gate
    we accompanied him thither
But WE were back again
    before midnight had come.

III

How vague and vast
 the desolate moorland grass,
And the white willows—
 how sad their whispering.
The heavy frost
 of this mid-November
Is with us all the way
 out through the distant suburbs.
At last, on all four sides
 there are no human dwellings,
Only lofty tomb-mounds
 rise in their gloomy grandeur.
Because of this our horses
 look at the sky and neigh.
Because of this the wind
 moans sadly to himself.
When once the deep vault
 has finally been sealed,
For a thousand years
 he will never see the dawn.
For a thousand years
 he will never see the dawn—
Intelligence and wisdom
 alike availed him nothing.
Presently those who have
 accompanied him hither
Each one by himself
 will return to his own home.
Family and kinsmen
 may still feel some grief—

Some of the others
        may already have been singing!
Of death and passing
        what can one say but this:
"Give up your body:
        become one with the hillside."

On Being Detained
at Kuei-lin by Contrary Winds

Through the Fifth Month of the Year
Keng-tzu (A.D. 400), while
Returning Home from the Capital

I

Ever on and on,
    the long return journey—
Reckoning the days
    I long for my old dwelling.
My first joy will be
    to see my parents' faces,
A second joy will be
    to visit with my brothers.
Our boat with rhythmic oars
    skirted bays and headlands,
As I pointed out the views
    all the way to Hsi-yü.
Rugged and perilous—
    the river and the mountains,
The returning voyager
    heeded the path ahead.
A south wind arose
    contrary to my mind,

So shipping the rudder
      we wait at the end of the lake.
Tall undergrowth extends
      limitless in the distance
Only catalpa trees
      stand out in scattered groves.
Who would say now
      that our journey should be long?
When I can clearly see
      more than a hundred *li*! [1]
Straining my eyes
      I recognize the Southern Range
And sigh in vain
      wondering when I'll reach it.

II

People have always sighed
      at the vicissitudes of travel—
I for the first time
      have learned them for myself.
Mountains and rivers—
      what a vast expanse they are,
With winds and waters
      hard to put our trust in.
Tumultuous waves
      clamour towards the heavens,
And the enduring wind
      knows no time of resting.
After long voyaging
      I yearn for my place of birth;
Why am I constrained
      to tarry here so long?

As I think quietly
      how good are my woods and gardens,
The ways of men
      are easy to leave behind.
The years before me
      cannot be very many—
Let me follow my heart
      and never doubt again.

[1] *Ordinarily I have translated the word "li" as "mile" for purely euphonic reasons. Here, however, "li" must be retained, since it is a distance of only roughly a third of a mile. Kuei-lin must have been somewhere down the river not far from Hu-k'ou, a place from which he could see Mt. Lu, often called the Southern Range (Nan-ling) or the Southern Mountain (Nan-shan).*

Written on Passing through Ch'ü-a[1]

After Being Appointed Adjutant for a Garrison Commander

In my boyhood years I dwelt beyond affairs,
And expressed my feelings only with brush and lute.
Wearing coarse hemp I was glad and self-contained:
And though "often hungry"[2] was ever serenely joyful.
But the time came when I had to go,
And drive my chariot along the avenues.[3]
Throwing aside my staff I ordered court robes made,
Temporarily estranged from my fields and gardens.
Far into the distance the lonely boat departed—
Continuous and constant the thought of returning home.
And my journeyings were very far indeed—
I climbed and traversed more than a thousand miles.
When my eyes grew weary of the strangeness of distant
roads
Then my heart would dwell on my own hills and valleys.
Gazing at the clouds I would envy the flying birds,
Staring at the waters I would envy the swimming fish.
Since such REAL[4] thoughts have been in me from the
start,
Who says that I'm ensnared in bonds of form and act?
Rather, for the present, I shift with the cosmic changes,
But shall in the end return to the abode of Master Pan.[5]

---

[1] *The modern Tan-yang-hsien in An-hui, south of Nanking, and some miles inland from the south bank of the Yangtze.*

² *Allusion to* ANALECTS, XI, 18, *"The Master said, Hui comes very near to it. He is often empty." Yen Hui was Confucius' favourite disciple—the one who had come nearest to realizing the supreme virtue, Love (*JEN*) or Goodness as translated by Waley. "Often empty" is interpreted in various ways—hard up, in want, empty of vanity, etc. But T'ao Ch'ien seems to use it in the sense of "often hungry"; cf. especially line 3 on p. 112.*

³ *i.e. in the Capital.*

⁴ *i.e. pertaining to the Tao.*

⁵ *i.e. Pan Ku, a mythical creator: Nature.*

Written in the Seventh Month of the Year Hsin-chou (A.D. 401)

While Passing T'u-k'ou[1] in the Night on my Way back to Chiang-ling for my Vacation

Living in retirement
    for more than thirty years,
At last I grew
    remote from the world's affairs.
Verse and calligraphy
    but confirmed me in this course,
Among my woods and gardens
    I had no worldly feelings.
How did I come
    to abandon this and go
Far far away
    to Ching-chou in the West?[2]
Now when the autumn moon
    strikes across the oars
At the river-bank
    I bid my friends farewell.
A cooling wind
    rises as darkness falls
And the night prospect
    is clear with an empty brilliance.
Glowing in splendour
    broad is the vault of Heaven,
Gleaming in radiance
    the smoothness of the stream.

Thinking of my long journey
    I cannot get to sleep,
And in the depth of night
    pace up and down alone.
What do I care
    about singing a Song of Shang, [3]
I am only filled with longing
    to go back to ploughing.
Renouncing my cap of office
    I will return to my old home
Never more entangled
    with love for high position.
I will nourish my REAL self
    under my gates and thatch
And by doing this
    be all the better known. [4]

[1] *T'u-k'ou, now called Chin-k'ou, is on the Yangtze, a few miles upstream from Hankow. It is in Hu-pei.*

[2] *Another name for Chiang-ling in Hu-pei, on the north bank of the Yangtze.*

[3] *In the HUAI-NAN TZU, Chap. IX, it is related that a poor man named Ning Ch'i was feeding oxen under a cart and while doing so beat time upon their horns and sang a song of Shang. Duke Huan of Ch'i (mid-seventh century B.C.) happened to hear him and was so struck with what his singing revealed of his character that he sent for him and subsequently made him a minister at his court. In alluding to this story T'ao Ch'ien wishes to imply that he does not desire to attract the attention of anyone who might recommend him for further official service.*

Songs of Shang were evidently some sort of ancient classical music which the Duke would not have expected a humble individual like Ning Ch'i to know.

[4] *cf. Horace's "Exegi monumentum aere perenrius"*

In the First Month of Spring of the Year K'uei-mao (A.D. 403)

I Think with Longing of an Old Family Estate

I

Long ago I heard of the Southern Acres
But in those years I never really trod them.
Since it is possible to be "often hungry"[1]
Labours of spring may not be avoided.
At the first light of dawn I harnessed my chariot—
No sooner had I started than my thoughts were there
                                                before me.
Birds played around me rejoicing in the springtime
While a cool morning breeze bade farewell to winter.
Bamboos of the cold season shade the tangled creekbed—
Indeed this place is uninhabited and far.
Like the old man who weeded with his staff[2]
I have come a long long way not to return again.
For he found the Truth scorning common knowledge,
The secret that he guarded had depth past comprehension.

II

The Ancient Master left[3] to us a teaching—
"Grieve at the Tao and not at poverty."[4]
Gazing aloft it is far and hard to reach[5]
All the more I wish to keep on striving towards it.
Holding the plough, I rejoice in the season's labours,
And with jokes and laughter encourage my fellow
                                                workers.
The level fields receive and welcome the wind from far,

And healthy sprouts thrill at the spring's return.
Although it is too soon to estimate the harvest
Going about my work I am glad of many things.
Ploughing and sowing we stop to rest at times,
And no one coming by inquires about the crossing.[6]
When the sun sinks we all go home together
And with jugs of wine I recompense my neighbours.
When, with a long-drawn sigh, I close my rustic gate,
It is good, belonging to the folk of the dykes and fields.

[1] *Allusion to Yen Hui, see note 2 on p. 109.*
[2] *A reference to the ANALECTS: "Once when Tzu-lu was following (the Master) he fell behind and met an old man carrying a basket slung over his staff. Tzu-lu asked him, saying, Sir, have you seen my Master? The old man said, You who*

> *With your four limbs do not toil,*
> *Who do not sift the five grains,*

who is your master? And with that he planted his staff in the ground and began weeding, while Tzu-lu stood by with his hands pressed together.

He kept Tzu-lu for the night, killed a fowl, prepared a dish of millet for his supper and introduced him to his two sons. Tzu-lu said, It is not right to refuse to serve one's country. The laws of age and youth may not be set aside. And how can it be right for a man to set aside the duty that binds minister to prince, or in his desire to maintain his own integrity, to subvert the Great Relationship? A gentleman's service to his country consists in his doing such right as he can. That the Way does not prevail, he knows well enough beforehand.

Next day Tzu-lu went on his way and reported what had happened. The Master said, He is a recluse, and told Tzu-lu to go back and visit him again. But on arriving at the place he found that the old man had gone away."

(Waley, ANALECTS, XVIII, 7.)

T'ao Ch'ien was fond of comparing himself to such hermits, cf. p. 123, line 18.
[3] *Confucius.*
[4] *". . . a gentleman's anxieties concern the progress of the Way; he has no anxiety concerning poverty."*   *(Waley, ANALECTS, XV, 31.)*
[5] *"Yen Hui said with a deep sigh, The more I strain my gaze up towards it*

113

[Love, Goodness], the higher it soars. The deeper I bore down into it, the harder it becomes. I see it in front; but suddenly it is behind. Step by step the Master skilfully lures one on. He has broadened me with culture, restrained me with ritual. Even if I wanted to stop, I could not. Just when I feel that I have exhausted every resource, something seems to rise up, standing out sharp and clear. Yet though I long to pursue it, I can find no way of getting to it at all."

(Waley, ANALECTS, IX, 10.)

⁶ *Ch'ang-chü and Chieh-ni were two hermits who had "retired from their generation". Confucius on one of his journeys happened to pass by where they were working in the fields and sent Tzu-lu to ask them where a river that lay ahead could be forded. The two men refused to reply, and upbraided Tzu-lu for serving a master who persisted in trying to change and uplift the world instead of retiring from it as they had done (cf. note 3 on p. 124).*

This passage of the ANALECTS is much alluded to in Chinese literature, and "to seek the crossing" is used with various connotations; but here T'ao Ch'ien simply means that the strenuous and energetic who would rise in the world and try to better it, never come to him for advice or to discuss their plans with him—that he has renounced the way of life of a Confucius, with all its earnest striving, and like Ch'ang-chü and Chieh-ni has given up the world and lost himself among the simple people of the countryside.

On Returning Home

Until recent days I lived in the Capital,
And have come home again after six years' absence.
Now that today I am back again at last
I am sick at heart and grieve at many things.
Dykes and boundary paths [1] have not changed at all
But houses and buildings differ here and there.
As I make the rounds through the ancient village,
Not many still remain of the older people.
Retracing step by step the footsteps of the past
There are places where I feel overwhelmed with deep
                                                    emotion.
Life's mirage flows past in less than a hundred years,
Hot and cold seasons chasing each other round,
Yet all my fear is that Great Creation [2] should run dry
Before my strength and spirit have altogether faded.
Lay it aside! Do not think of it again,
Rather be happy and flourish a cup of wine.

[1] *Raised paths between the rice fields.*
[2] *Literally: "Great Transformations or Permutations", the constant spontaneous self-creation of the universe. He fears only, that is, that the world may somehow come to an end before he has lived his life to the full and used up all his strength.*

Written for his Paternal First Cousin

Ching-yuan in the Twelfth Month of the Year K'uei-mao[1]

I stay my steps
    under the rustic gate,
Dwelling afar
    and cut off from the world.
No one knows
    about my daily doings,
The thornwood doors
    are always closed by day.
Chill is the wind
    of the evening of the year,
All-enveloping
    the snows that fall all day—
Though I incline my ear
    there is not the slightest sound,
And my eyes can see
    nothing but purest whiteness.
The sinewy winds
    invade my sleeves and collar,
Wine gourd and rice basket
    decline to be brought out often.
Desolate and silent
    are my empty rooms,
Utterly without
    anything to cheer me.
Scanning line by line
    books of a thousand years,
From time to time I find
    tales of heroic virtue.

To such high principles
I cannot aspire
But I do know how
"to bear adversity".[2]
Though, alas, I cannot follow
the example of P'ing-chin,[3]
At least I understand
how to enjoy my leisure.
To express my thought
has taken more than a word,
But now no one can sever
the bond that is between us.

[1] *The year K'uei-mao corresponds roughly to A.D. 403, but the greater part of the twelfth month of it falls in January 404.*

[2] *The Agony of Ch'ên, see note 1 on p. 127.*

[3] *Kung-sun Hung (died 121 B.C.), courtesy title Chi-shao. He was born to poverty in the feudal state of Hsieh in what is now Shantung, and herded swine by the seashore. At the age of forty he began to study the SPRING AND AUTUMN ANNALS with their various commentaries.*

The Emperor Wu of the Former Han dynasty (regn. 140–86 B.C.) heard of him and appointed him a Doctor of Confucian Learning (at the Capital), but he excused himself and returned to his home. During the Yüan Kuang era (134–128 B.C.) he was summoned to the Capital to take the official examina-tion in classical learning, and took the highest honours. The Emperor again appointed him Doctor of Confucian Learning, and during the Yüan So era (128–122 B.C.) he rose to be a Minister of State, and was enfeoffed with the title of Marquis of P'ing-chin.

At court he was famous for his frequent orations and harangues on moral subjects, and it is to this reputation as a Confucian moralist that T'ao Ch'ien alludes here.

On Crossing Cash Creek[1]

*In the Third Month of the Year I-szu
(A.D. 405) while on a Mission to
the Capital after Being Appointed
Adjutant on the Staff of the
Chien-wei Guards*

Since last I was here and trod upon this ground
The months and years make up quite a pile.
Morning and evening I gaze at the hills and streams
Everything about them is as it was of old.
A fine rain washes the lofty woods
While whirling winds play with the feet of the clouds.
Seeing how these things all have remained the same
I see that constancy has not vanished from the world.
And this person that is I—what am I about
Striving so hard to go away from here?
Just as the bodily form has its fixed fashioning,
So one's early emotions cannot be effaced.
Every day in dreams I see my fields and gardens.
How can I possibly remain away for long?
Eternally I long for the boat that will take me home,
For truly I belong there among the frosty cedars.

---

[1] *Ch'ien-hsi, the modern Mei-ken-ho in Anhui. It flows northward into the
Yangtze between T'ung-ling and Kuei-ch'ih.*

On My House Burning Down

In the Sixth Month of the
Year Wu-shen
(A.D. 408)

My thatched cottage stood close to the narrow lane,
For which I had been glad to leave an official mansion.
In the first month of summer a long high wind arose
And my woods and buildings suddenly turned to ashes.
In the whole compound not a single roof remains,
My lodging is a boat moored before the gate.
High are the heavens of the new autumn evening,
Lofty and serene, the moon is almost full.
Fruit and garden greens have begun to grow again
But the frightened birds have not yet returned.
I stand alone at midnight pondering far-off things
And my troubled gaze roams over the Nine Heavens.[1]
When I wore a topknot I was aloof and independent—[2]
Then I suddenly left home and was gone for forty years.
Bodily form and features changed as time went on
But in my spirit-mansion I was ever at peace alone.
For constancy and strength there was a solid basis
Beside which jade and stone are not firm at all.
I like to think back to the time of Tung-hu [3]
When people could leave grain in the open overnight.
To drum upon one's belly in complete insouciance [4]
Just rising in the morning and lying down at night,
I have never experienced anything like that
So let me just get on with watering my garden.

¹ *A very ancient traditional expression explained in a variety of ways in various texts, but the simplest is the Eight Directions, N., NE., E., SE., etc., and the zenith or centre.*

² *Until the capping ceremony at their initiation to manhood at twenty, boys wore their hair in twin topknots known as "tuft-horns" (TSUNG CHIOH).*

³ *Reference to a passage in the HUAI-NAN TZU, "In the time of Tung-hu Chi Tzu the passers-by along the highways would not glean grain left along them, but would leave it overnight at the very edges of the fields."*

⁴ *Allusion to a passage in the CHUANG TZU, "Now, in the time of Ho Hsü Tzu the people when at rest did not know what they did, when they walked they did not know where they were going. When they filled their mouths to feed they were happy, and roamed about drumming on their bellies."*

(CHUANG TZU, Chap. IX.)

Written on the Ninth Day
of the Ninth Month

Of the Year I-yu
(A.D. 409)

Slowly, slowly,
    the autumn draws to its close.
Cruelly cold
    the wind congeals the dew.
Vines and grasses
    will not be green again—
The trees in my garden
    are withering forlorn.
The pure air
    is cleansed of lingering lees
And mysteriously,
    the Heaven's realms are high.
Nothing is left
    of the spent cicada's song,
A flock of geese
    goes crying down the sky.
The myriad transformations
    unravel one another
And human life
    how should it not be hard?
From ancient times
    there was none but had to die,
Remembering this
    scorches my very heart.

What is there I can do
    to assuage this mood?
Only enjoy myself
    drinking my unstrained wine.
I do not know
    about a thousand years,
Rather let me make
    this morning last forever.

On Harvesting the First Rice

In the Western Field in the Ninth Month of the Year Keng-hsü (A.D. 410)

Although human life must conform to Tao
Clothing and food are surely aspects of it.
For who can completely disregard such things
And in so doing attain to happiness? [1]
In spring I attended to the usual tasks
And now my harvest is quite considerable.
Going out at dawn I spent a little toil,
When the sun went down I brought the grain back home.
Along the hillside paths the frosty dew was thick
And the wind's breath was prematurely chill.
The farmer's life cannot but be hard—
He cannot possibly escape such sufferings [2]
Let the four limbs be weary as they please,
Just so no sudden calamities arrive!
Having bathed myself I rest beneath the eaves
And a pot of wine relaxes face and feelings.
Afar, afar over a thousand years
I sense a kinship with the hermits Chü and Ni. [3]
All I desire is to go on like this,
I do not sorrow that I must labour in the fields.

---

[1] *As the Taoist philosophers claimed that the Ancients did, before the Sages "came to worry them with ritual and music, and dangled charity and duty to one's neighbour before them". cf. note 2 on p. 143.*

[2] *See p. 55, last line, and note 2.*

³ *"Ch'ang-chü and Chieh-ni were working as plough-mates together. Master K'ung [Confucius], happening to pass that way, told Tzu-lu to go and ask them where the river could be forded. Ch'ang-chü said, Who is it for whom you are driving? Tzu-lu said, For K'ung-Ch'iu. He said, What, K'ung-Ch'iu of Lu? Tzu-lu said, Yes, he. Ch'ang-chü said, In that case he already knows where the ford is. Tzu-lu then asked Chieh-ni. Chieh-ni said, Who are you? He said, I am Tzu-lu. Chieh-ni said, You are a follower of K'ung-Ch'iu of Lu, are you not? He said, That is so. Chieh-ni said, Under Heaven there is none that is not swept along by the same flood. Such is the world and who can change it? As for you, instead of following one who flees from this man and that, you would do better to follow one who shuns this whole generation of men. And with that he went on covering the seed.*

"Tzu-lu went and told his master, who said ruefully, One cannot herd with birds and beasts. If I am not to be a man among other men, then what am I to be? If the Way prevailed under Heaven, I should not be trying to alter things."

(Waley, ANALECTS, XVIII, 6) cf. Introduction, pp. 32 and 40.

Written in the Eighth Month of the Year Ping ch'en (A.D. 416)

On Going to Take in the Harvest at the Outlying Farm at Hsia-sun

Dwelling in poverty relying on reaping and sowing
I spent my strength on a plot by the Eastern Woods.
But last spring's bitter labour is not worth mentioning
Compared to my constant fear of losing what I longed for.
The field-hands too feeling the Fall at hand
Raise their voices in harmony with me
Hungry, they look forward to their first bellyful,
They tie their belts and so await the cockcrow.
Then, lifting the oars we cross the level lake,
And follow the turnings of the verdant valley.
Far in the depths among the tangled forests
The monkeys' cries sound faint and sorrowful.
The sorrowing wind loved the quiet night,
Now the woodland birds rejoice at the break of day.
Since I first began to make the journey here
Quite a few star-fires have crumbled into nothing.
Youth has departed but though I now am old
This is one matter that I can still attend to:
I salute from afar the Old Man with the Staff—[1]
And only wish that I could go and visit him.

[1] See note 2 on p. 113.

125

I

Of the Myriad Tribes each has some reliance,
But the Lonely Cloud alone[1] has no support.
Dimly, dimly, it fades into the sky—
No faintest glimmer will be seen of it again.
The light of dawn parts the mists of night,
And flocks of birds go flying up together.
Slowly, slowly, they fly out from the woods
Where they will return before it is yet evening.
When it takes so much strength just to keep in the old rut
How can he possibly escape being cold and hungry?
If friends know this and will not stand by him
Enough of them—he need feel no sorrow.

[1] *Symbolizes the poor scholar.*

II

Sharp and chill
    the year is at its evening,
I lay out summer clothes
    to sun on the front verandah.
In the southern garden
    nothing green is left,
And withered branches
    fill the northern orchard.
I have tipped the jar
    till the very dregs are gone,
Peering into the kitchen
    I see no hint of smoke.
Poems and histories
    are piled about my seat
Even by sundown
    I have had no time to study.
Living thus alone
    is not the Agony of Ch'ên[1]
But I have resentments
    that will come out in words.
What can I rely on
    to assuage my feelings?
That many ancient sages
    were situated so!

[1] "*In Ch'ên supplies fell short and his followers became so weak that they could not drag themselves on to their feet. Tzu-lu came to the Master and said indignantly, Is it right that even gentlemen should be reduced to such straits? The Master said, A gentleman can withstand hardships; it is only the small man who, when submitted to them, is swept off his feet.*"

                      (Waley, *ANALECTS, XV*, 1.)

See note 2 on p. 117.

III

Jung when he was old
    wore a rope for a girdle [1]
But he was happy
    and played upon the lute.
Master Yüan's shoes
    always showed his heels [2]
And Tsêng Tzu's clear singing
    released the tones of Shang. [3]
Though Shun the Emperor
    left us long ago
Still poor scholars
    tried to emulate him. [4]
The sleeve of Tsêng Tzu's robe
    scarcely hid his elbow
And even onion soup
    he could not always serve.
Master Yüan did not forget
    that he once went clad in furs [5]
But to get them wrongfully
    was not what he desired [6]
Tzu-kung might talk
    as much as he pleased—
It was simply that he could not
    see within his heart. [7]

---

[1] *See note 2 on p. 64.*

[2] *Master Yüan; a disciple of Confucius referred to in the* ANALECTS *as Yüan Ssu (courtesy title Tzu-ssu), but elsewhere sometimes called Yüan Hsien. Retiring yet firm by nature, his dwelling place had hinges of wattle and windows made of sections of an earthenware jar. When he straightened his cap the chin-straps would come off; when he adjusted his lapels his elbows would show; and when he tied his shoes his heels would stick out. Tzu-kung (another*

of Confucius' disciples) passed by and asked if he were ill. Yüan replied: "The lack of money is called poverty, but to study the Way without being able to put it into practice is called illness. Poverty such as mine is not illness."

³ In the CHUANG TZU it is related that when Tsêng Tzu, a disciple of Confucius, was living in Wei, his elbows showed whenever he adjusted his lapels, and his heels stuck out when he tied his shoes. Yet he wandered unconcerned trailing his staff on the ground, and the sound of his singing filled Heaven and Earth.

⁴ "The master said, Sublime were Shun and Yü! All that is under Heaven was theirs, yet they remained aloof from it." Yao, Shun, and Yü were three mythical culture heroes by Confucius' time historicized as emperors and placed before the earliest known dynasty, the Hsia (traditional dates 2205–1766 B.C.). Like Yao, who sought him out while he was dwelling in obscurity, and resigned the empire to him, Shun set aside his own son who was unworthy, and conferred the empire upon Yü. I suppose that it is this modesty which T'ao Ch'ien has in mind as the quality which the poor scholars had in common.

⁵ Tradition has it that when Confucius was minister of justice in the state of Lu he made Yüan superintendent of his household.

⁶ Yüan was noted for his scrupulousness. In the ANALECTS (VI, 3) we read: "When Yüan Ssu was made a governor, he was given an allowance of nine hundred measures of grain, but declined it. The Master said, Surely you could find people who would be glad of it among your neighbours or in your village?" And again (ibid., XIV, 1): "Yüan Ssu asked about compunction. The Master said, When a country is ruled according to the Way [the gentleman] accepts rewards. But when a country is not ruled according to the Way, he shows compunction in regard to rewards."

⁷ Tzu-kung's rude question (and the reason for his discomforture) came from the fact that he did not realize, or failed to remember, that Yuan's poverty and hence his ragged appearance were due to his unbending scrupulousness and not to any lack of capacity.

IV

Happy though poor—guarding humility,
An old example is that of Ch'ien Lou.[1]
Offered high rank, he would not accept the honour;
Offered rich gifts, he would not become involved[2]
Once on a morning his span of life was spent,
And his worn-out clothing could not hide his body.
Of course people saw his great extremity,
But the Way was not at stake and
    therefore no one grieved.[3]
Since he lived is nigh on a thousand years,
And still his like has never yet been seen.
To be born in the morning possessed of
    Love and Faith
And die at evening, what more could one desire?

[1] *Ch'ien Lou, a somewhat legendary figure of the spring and autumn period, contemporary of Confucius. Tradition says that Duke Kung of Lu, bearing of his wisdom, wished to make him a minister of state in his dukedom, but he declined. Prince Wei of Ch'i invited him to become privy councillor at his court, but he did not accept. After that, every time an enemy invaded Ch'i, the prince would come on foot to consult with him and as a result escape the danger, while no one in the country knew quite how. He was extremely poor, and when he died his coat did not cover his body so that Tsêng Tzu (one of the disciples of Confucius) said: "If we put it on him diagonally it would reach", whereupon his wife answered: "Even if it would cover him if you put it on diagonally, I would rather have it on him straight and not long enough! My husband was not diagonal (oblique) by nature, and now that he is dead he would not wish to have anything diagonal about him."*

Tsêng Hsi could think of no reply, and proceeded with the ceremonial wailing for the dead. After finishing the bewailment he asked the widow what post-humous title she planned to give to her husband. She replied that she had chosen the name "K'ang" (abundant health, peace and plenty). Tsêng Tzu said, "when the Master was alive he never had enough food to eat or clothes to wear, and now that he is dead his robe will not even cover his body! What happiness is in all this that you should call him K'ang?"

She answered: "You yourself once wished to appoint him a minister of state. He declined and did not accept the position, but here was more than enough honour. Again you once wished to make him a present of thirty chung of grain. This too he would not take, but was he not more than rich enough [by virtue of having been offered it]? All the flat and flavourless things under Heaven were sweet to the Master. He was content with a humble position in the world, did not fret at poverty and lowliness or envy the rich and noble. He sought Love and attained Love, he sought what was right and found it. Surely it is fitting that I should call him K'ang."

[2] The exchange of valuable presents between friends was customary in ancient China, but Ch'ien Lou, knowing that he could not afford to return things of like value, refused expensive gifts even though his rich and influential admirers knowing his poverty would not have expected any return.

[3] "The Master said, A Knight whose heart is set upon the Way, but who is ashamed of wearing shabby clothes and eating coarse food, is not worth calling into counsel." (Waley, ANALECTS, IV, 9.)

See also note 4 on p. 113.

V

The snow lay deep
 before Yüan An's door,
But he was "far away"
 and it did not concern him.[1]
And when Duke Yüan
 saw the contributions [2]
On that very day
 he resigned from office.
A bed of straw
 was always warm enough,
And fresh gathered yams
 were good enough for breakfast.
What they suffered
 was the REAL pain,[3]
Hunger and cold
 they did not fear at all.
Poverty and wealth
 will always war within us,[4]
But when the Tao prevails
 there are no anxious faces.
Utmost moral power
 will crown the village entrance
And purest chastity
 shine in the western gateway.

[1] *In the Chin History it is related that there was a great fall of snow in Lo-yang. The Governor of the District passed by Yüan An's door and seeing no footprints in the snow thought that he might have died. Going in he found Yüan An sitting at his ease. When he asked him why he was so unconcerned he replied: "When there is a blizzard like this one everybody would be equally hard put to it to get enough to eat; how could I think of bothering anyone!"*

² *Duke Yüan was noble but poor, he took office and some of his friends took up a collection for him, whereupon he resigned.*

³ *i.e. the pain of realizing that the Tao does not prevail in the world. According to Confucius the Gentleman's only concern should be with the Way (Tao), his own circumstances (wealth or poverty) should mean nothing to him.*

⁴ *In the HAN FEI-TZU the following passage occurs: "Tzu-hsia [a disciple of Confucius] said, Going within, I saw the Right proclaimed by the Former Kings; going abroad, I saw wealth and high position, and these two were always locked in combat in my breast, and therefore I grew lean. But now that the Right proclaimed by the Former Kings has won the battle I am fat again."*

VI

Chang Chung-wei[1] loved his poor abode,
Where artemisia grew round about the house.
He dwelt secluded, cut off from social pleasures,
But in making poems he was very skilful.
In all the world there was none who knew him,
Except one man, a certain Liu Kung.
Why did such a scholar have to be so lonely?
Surely, because few had much in common with him.
Resolute in this, he delighted in his work;
His joy did not concern either success or failure.
In friendly intercourse I have always been most clumsy,
But I wish I'd had the chance to know a man like him!

[1] *Chang Chung-wei wrote excellent prose and also verse and prose-poems.
He dwelt all his life in poverty and simplicity. Artemisia grew all around his
house, where people never came. He kept his gate closed and nourished his inner
nature. No one among his contemporaries knew him except a certain Liu Kung.*

Lingering Clouds

The lingering clouds make me think of a dear friend. When the wine cups are filled full of new wine, when the garden displays its first bloom, and I cannot have his company, I sigh and rest, pulling my coat close about me.

1

Lowering, lowering, the lingering clouds,
Drizzling, drizzling, the seasonal rains.
The Eight Directions[2] are all alike in twilight,
The level roads all but impassable.
Quietly I go out to the east verandah
And nurse my cup of spring wine all alone.
When my good friend seems so far away
I scratch my head and stand dejectedly.

2

Lingering clouds, lowering, lowering,
Seasonal rains, drizzling, drizzling,
The Eight Directions are all alike in twilight,
The level land has turned into a river.
But wine I have, wine I have,
Leisurely I drink it by the eastern window,
For the friend whom I am longing for,
Cannot be reached by boat or chariot.

3

Now the trees in the eastern garden
Twigs and branches have again put forth.
I too will hasten to be with friends and kinsfolk
And by so doing elevate my feelings.
People also have a saying—
"The days and months are on the march"
Would that I could sit face to face with you.
And settle the problems of our daily life.

4

Fluttering, fluttering, the flying birds,
Settle on the branches in my courtyard.
Gathering in their wings they stop at leisure,
And harmonize together tunefully.
Surely many other people
Are thinking of you constantly,
But when I cannot have you with me
Oh, how resentment burns my heart.

[1] *See Introduction, p. 19.*
[2] *The four cardinal points of the compass and the quarters.*

The Revolution of the Seasons

This poem is based directly upon section 25 of Book XI of the ANALECTS, in which Confucius asks four of his disciples, ". . . At present you are out of office and feel that your merits are not recognized. Now supposing someone were to recognize your merits, what employment would you choose?"

The first three men all made choices which implied ambition for power and high rank, but Tsêng Hsi, the fourth, made quite a different choice:

"[the Master said] Tien, what about you? The notes of the zithern he was softly fingering died away; he put it down, rose and replied, saying, I fear my words will not be so well chosen as those of the other three. The Master said, What harm is there in that? All that matters is that each should name his desire.

"Tsêng Hsi said, At the end of spring when the making of the Spring Clothes has been completed, to go with five times six newly-capped youths, and six times seven uncapped boys, perform the lustration in the River Yi, take the air at the Rain Dance Altars, and then go home singing. The Master heaved a deep sigh and said, I am with Tien." (Waley, ANALECTS, XI, 25.)

T'ao Ch'ien's whole poem is in the spirit of Tsêng Hsi's reply, which is surely the most lyrical passage in the ANALECTS. But in his prose preface he alludes to the fact that his morning excursion was made alone, so that his pleasure was not quite perfect.

The turning of the seasons has brought us to late spring, and now that our Spring Robes have been completed and the prospect is fine, I go forth alone to enjoy it with only my shadow for company, which gives me mingled feelings of joy and regret.

1

Inexorably swift, the turning of the seasons,
Grandly majestic is this fair morning.
I put on my Spring Robes[1]
And go for a while to the eastern hill.
The mountains shed their lingering haze
But the sky is veiled in a light overcast.
There comes a wind out of the south
Brushing the new sprouts with its wings.

2

Wide, wide, the quiet shallows
I rinse my mouth and wash my hands,[2]
Far, far the distant view,
Filled with joy I gaze upon it.
People also have a saying,
"One is soon content with that which suits the heart",
And so I flourish a cup of wine—
Enjoy myself in utter self-content.

3

Gazing afar, at the centre of the stream,
I think of the Yi River long ago,[3]
When uncapped boys and youths performed[4] together,
And then returned while singing leisurely.
I love the quietness of that,
Sleeping and waking I wish to live with it,
Only, alas, I live in another age,
It is far away, and I cannot reach it.

This morning and this evening
I will rest in my retreat;
Flowers and herbs in separate rows—
Woods and bamboo groves screening it in.
The Pure Lute lies across my couch;
Of unstrained wine there is half a jug.
That the ancient sages[5] cannot be with me
Only I can know how sorely I regret it.

[1] *Allusion to the passage in the ANALECTS, "when the making of the Spring Clothes has been completed". Probably special ritual attire for the ceremony, but T'ao Ch'ien probably knew no more about it than we do.*

[2] *An allusion to the lustration ceremony in the quotation from the ANALECTS.*

[3] *A river that rises in Central Shantung and flows straight south, its waters ultimately reaching the Yangtze.*

[4] *Probably ritual dances with singing, all associated with the lustration ceremonies at the river.*

[5] *The text says quite literally "the Yellow Emperor (Huang Ti) and T'ang Yao"; both legendary Emperors or culture heroes of ancient Chinese mythology.*

The Flowering Tree

A flowering tree puts us in mind of the swift approach of
old age. The days and months have flown past, and now it
is already the festival of the Ninth Day of the Ninth Month.[1]
And even should one hear the Way when one's hair is
bound in childish horn-locks, one's hair will be white ere
one be perfect in it.

I

Bright, bright, the flowering tree,
That's taken root upon this spot.
The blossoms that it shone with in the morning,
It will have lost before the night has fallen.
Human life is like a sojourning
Yet for melancholy there is time to spare.
Brooding long in silence on these things
My heart is filled with bitterness and grief.

2

Bright, bright, the flowering tree,
Upon this spot it has taken root.
Densely its blossoms open in the morning
A pity, in the evening they are gone.
To be firm or fragile is our own affair:
No gateways lead to doom or happiness.
What can we rely on save the Tao?
What is there to sustain us save the Good?

Alas, alas, my little children
That have inherited this poor estate.
The passing years have slipped away
Without my adding to my patrimony.
Striving for *that*, I cannot put it from me;
Resigned to *this*, I might grow daily richer.
Such are the thoughts I bear within my breast;
Sick to the heart, all's malady within me.

4

The Ancient Master left to us a teaching
That I will ever keep before my mind.
"If at forty he is still unknown,
There is no need to stand in awe of him."[2]
Come, let me oil my famous chariot,
Let me whip up my famous thoroughbreds,
Although a thousand miles is a long way,
How can I dare not to accomplish it?

[1] *See note 1 on p. 51.*
[2] *From the ANALECTS: "The Master said, Respect the young. How do you know that they will not one day be all that you are now? But if a man has reached forty or fifty and nothing has been heard of him, then I grant there is no need to respect him."* (Waley, ANALECTS, IX, 22).

An Exhortation to Agriculture

1

Long, long ago in High Antiquity,
When the people had been first created,
They were proud and self-sufficient—
Guarded simplicity and the Truth[1] was in them.
But when cleverness and artifice arose,[2]
There was no way to meet their daily needs.[3]
Who was there to help in such a case?
Verily, they relied upon a Wise Man.

2

And that wise man, who was he?
None other than the Millet Sovereign.[4]
What was the help he rendered unto them?
Verily, he taught them how to plant and sow.
Shun[5] the Emperor ploughed with his own hand,
And Yü the Great,[6] he also tilled the soil.
And the ancient Institutes of Chou[7]
Put food production first among the Eight Depart-
ments.

3

Clear, clear, the sounds that call us,
Lush, lush, the virgin soil.
Herbs and trees are blooming in profusion,
The gentle wind is pure and reverent.
Men and women busy everywhere
Vie with one another for an early start.
Mulberry girls fare forth before the dawn,
The farmer spent the night beside his plough.

Haste, for the season quickly will have passed
This perfect weather cannot last for ever.
Chi Ch'üeh's wife joined him in the fields [8]
And Chü and Chieh Ni [9] laboured side by side.
Seeing how these sages and wise people
Were diligent among their dykes and acres,
How much the less should all we common folk
"Sit with trailing robes and folded hands." [10]

5

The people's very life depends on diligence,
And if they are diligent they shall not suffer want.
Toiling, they can relax and be at peace,
And need beg for nothing at the evening of the year.
For him who has not laid aside ten bushels,
Cold and hunger will come hand in hand.
And when he looks about him at his neighbours,
How can he help but feel ashamed!

6

Confucius was so deep in Tao and virtue,
That it was wrong of Fan to trouble him, [11]
And Tung Chung-shu [12] so loved his lute and books,
That he never trod his fields and gardens.
But even could we transcend human toil,
And keep our footsteps upon such high paths,
Still it behoves us to adjust our rôles,
And reverently praise the beauty of its virtue.

[1] i.e. of the Tao.

[2] See note 1 on p. 123. A whole school of ancient Chinese philosophers, notably the Taoists, condemned all material progress.

[3] "When falsehood and artificiality had come into being, then people left the fundamental pursuits and pursued the unessential. Casting aside the labour of ploughing and husbandry, they applied themselves to the profits of awl and knife. Heaven knew that they would starve and therefore rained down grain...." (From the commentary on a passage in the HUAI-NAN TZU.)

[4] Hou Chi, the harvest god, associated with Yü the Great in the ANA-LECTS.

[5] Yao, Shun, and Yü are the most frequently mentioned of the Divine Sages of Antiquity, historicized as emperors.

[6] In the ANALECTS this is mentioned, and his name is coupled with that of the Millet Sovereign. Elsewhere he is the great Flood Subduer. Historicized, he is the founder of the Hsia dynasty. (cf. Waley, ANALECTS, Introduction.)

[7] That part of the ancient BOOK OF HISTORY (SHU CHING) relating to the Chou dynasty was so called. In one of its chapters, the HUNG FAN or Great Plan, under the heading of Agricultural Affairs, occurs a list of Eight Administrations (PA CHENG) which could be rendered Eight (Administrative) Departments.

[8] Allusion to a passage in the TSO CHUAN (commentary on the SPRING AND AUTUMN ANNALS of the state of Lu from 721–481 B.C.) Duke Hsi, thirty-third year. The passage runs as follows: "Once Chiu Chi, envoy of Duke Wen of Chin, was passing through Chi in the territory of Chin, when he saw a certain Chi Ch'üeh hoeing in the fields, his wife bringing a meal out to him, and the two treating each other with the same respect as is usual between host and guest. On his way back he took Chi Ch'üeh with him and said to Duke Wen, 'Respect is the gathering of all the virtues. He who knows how to give it must necessarily have virtue [inner power] and virtue is that by which the people are ruled. I beg that you will employ him.'"

[9] See note 3 on p. 124.

[10] Certain of the ancient Sage Kings were said to have ruled all under Heaven by merely arranging their robes, folding their hands and sitting facing the south. They ruled entirely through their inner power (virtue) and needed to do nothing more than that. Shun was one of these; nevertheless he sometimes ploughed,

hence, says T'ao Ch'ien, if even such a Divine Sage (who could rule by non-activity) did so, how much more should we who do not share his mystic power?

[11] "*Fan Ch'ih asked the Master to teach him about farming. The Master said, You had much better consult some old farmer. He asked to be taught about gardening. The Master said, You had much better go to some old vegetable-gardener.*" (Waley, ANALECTS, XIII, 4.)

[12] *Tung Chung-shu (c. 179–93 B.C.). In his youth he studied the SPRING AND AUTUMN ANNALS and their commentaries, and during the reign of Ching Ti (156–140 B.C.) was made a Doctor of Confucian Learning. He put down the blinds [of his house] and gave lectures and recitations. Disciples came and went all day until at the last he could scarcely see their faces, but still he would go on with his recitations with the utmost enthusiasm. For three years he never caught a glimpse of his garden.*

In Answer to the Adjutant P'ang

Written for him on the occasion of his passing through Hsün-yang on his way to the Capital from Chiang-ling to take his post as Adjutant in the Guards.

1

Under the rustic gate
I have my lute and books.
Playing it and reading them
Therein I take delight.
More good things I have besides—
I love my far-off dwelling,
In the morning watering the garden,
Evenings, lying at ease under my thatched roof.

2

The things which men treasure
Are not always really precious
And when they do not love the same things
How can they be intimate?
Just when I was seeking for companionship
I suddenly met the very man I longed for.
Joy filled my heart to overflowing
And the whole house up to the very rafters.

146

3

This friend of my heart
Is ever diligent in virtue.
I have sweet wine
Which I enjoy with him.
Now we discourse fine words
Now we compose new poems.
On any day when he is not here
How could I fail to think of him?

Appendix I

CHARACTERISTICS OF T'AO CH'IEN'S VERSE COMPARISONS

PERHAPS THE first thing that strikes the Western reader when he becomes acquainted with Chinese poetry is its prevailingly reflective or meditative mood. Except for the Elegies of Ch'u (see Introduction, p. 18) there is little vehemence or high passion to be found. This is partly due to the fact that personal and passionate love poems are all but non-existent. The Chinese seem to have felt even from before the Han dynasty that one's love life was better kept to oneself; that in any case it was unsuitable material for serious literature. So we do not find Chinese poets writing poems to ladies imploring them to be kind, or asserting that they will die or waste away if these do not relent. No doubt Chinese poets, too, often experienced such emotions, but they would have been ashamed to commit such sentiments to writing. In the same way the various Chinese religions and philosophies and Buddhism which came from India all lacked a personal God in the Christian or Islamic sense, and there was no Saviour or Mother of God, so that poems overflowing with passionate religious emotion are also quite exceptional. In all this T'ao Ch'ien was thoroughly typical and even a sort of ideal example. He never mentions women, though other poets wrote melancholy poems about neglected wives or concubines, descriptions of dancers, nymphs, or Imperial concubines. And his religion was not a burning faith but a philosophical attitude.

His poems are chiefly notable for their absolute naturalness and unpretentiousness. Literary allusions, the curse of later Chinese poetry, are seldom used, and those he does employ are simple and natural, almost inevitable. Personification, which is always a rare device in Chinese literature, he never uses. The seasons, the moon, heaven and earth, and so on, are occasionally personified, but never such abstractions as peace, hope, justice, etc. A verse like the following, for example, by Wu Chün (469–520) would be unimaginable coming from T'ao Ch'ien.

149

From what land has Spring just come,
Smoothing the waters, waking the plum to life?

His poems all have to do with his own personal life, his thoughts, his perceptions, or incidents he has witnessed. Or they may serve to set forth his ideals, as in the series, Songs of Poor Scholars. In this he is very close to Po Chü-i of the T'ang dynasty, who perhaps consciously followed him in writing simple, straightforward, self-revealing verse.

Apart from candour and simplicity, the most striking characteristic of his poems is their quiet tone and sense of gentle restraint. Like Li Po of the T'ang dynasty, he was a great lover of wine—they are perhaps the two outstanding alcoholics among all the Chinese poets, but even in his praise of wine T'ao Ch'ien shows his characteristic restraint. The difference between this and the passion and abandon of Li Po when writing on this subject should be very evident from the verses of the later poet three of which I give here for comparison.

I

Amidst the flowers
    a jug of wine—
I pour alone
    lacking companionship,
So raising the cup
    I invite the moon,
Then turn to my shadow
    which makes three people.
Because the moon
    does not know how to drink
My shadow merely
    follows my body.
The moon has brought the shadow
    to keep me company a while,
The practice of mirth
    should keep pace with spring.
I start a song
    and the moon begins to reel,
I rise and dance
    and the shadow moves grotesquely.
While I'm still conscious
    let's rejoice with one another,

After I'm drunk
    let each one go his way.
Let us bind ourselves for ever
    for passionless journeyings.
Let us swear to meet again
    far in the Milky Way.

II

If Heaven itself
    did not love wine,
Then no Wine Star
    would shine in the sky.
And if Earth also
    did not love wine,
Earth would have no such
    place as Wine Fountain.
Since Heaven and Earth
    do love wine.
That I too should love wine
    is no offence to Heaven.
Have I not heard
    that pure wine makes a Sage,
And even muddy wine
    can make a man wise?
If wise men and sages
    are already drinkers
What is the use
    of seeking gods and fairies?
With three cups
    I understand the great Way [Tao]
With one jar
    I am at one with Nature.
Only, the perceptions
    that one has while drunk,
Cannot be transmitted
    after one is sober.

III

In the third month
    the city of Hsien-yang—
Thousands of flowers
    at noon like brocade.
Who is able
    in spring to be sad alone?
Faced with this
    to drink is the shortest way.
Infinite things
    as well as short and long,
Alike have early been
    offered us by Creation.
A single cup
    may rank with life and death,
The myriad things
    are truly hard to fathom.
Once I am drunk
    losing Heaven and Earth,
Unsteadily
    I go to my lonely pillow.
Not to know
    that my self exists—
Of all my joys
    this is the highest.

Appendix II

PROBLEMS IN THE TRANSLATION
OF CHINESE POETRY

THE FIRST problem that confronts anyone who wishes to translate Chinese poetry lies in the nature of the language itself. Chinese is one of a group of languages, to which Tibetan and Siamese also belong, in which nearly all the words are simple monosyllables and in which tone or pitch and inflection are inherent in each word. In old Chinese the exceptions were very rare, and for practical purposes we may say that every word was an indeclinable monosyllable. A curious fact is the apparent universal trend among the languages of civilized nations in the direction of more and more simplicity—the wearing down of conjugations and declensions, the gradual elimination of case endings in nouns and adjectives, and of personal endings and moods in the verbs. Among the European languages this process has gone furthest in the case of English, in which the dative case no longer has any forms of its own and the accusative is found only in the pronouns him, her, them, etc.

Now, in Chinese this morphological development from the complex to the simple had already long before T'ao Ch'ien's time reached its limit. In the earliest literature some vestiges of case distinctions seem still to be traceable in the pronouns, and it is possible that the tenses and moods of verbs may have been distinguished by tones, or changes in the vowel or diphthong of the root, as is still the case in Tibetan. Such changes would not show up, of course, in an ideographic system of writing. But by T'ao Ch'ien's time Chinese had become a language in which each word was a simple monosyllable without any inflections whatever. The nouns had no cases, and no singular and plural; the verbs had no tenses, moods, or distinctions of person and number. These distinctions could be made, and in practice were made, whenever necessary or desirable—the plural of "that man" could be expressed by saying "that several man", "that many man", or "that class man". Actually there was, and is, only one pronoun for he, she, and it; the past and future tenses of "he go" could be expressed by using any of a number of adverbs of time—"he already go", "he hereafter go". But even in prose it was customary and always permissible to leave out such precise indications *whenever the writer believed that his meaning would be sufficiently clear from the context*; indeed, on occasion, writers were perhaps too much inclined to give themselves the benefit of the doubt in this regard. The result was that a great many passages in the early literature which seem to read well enough at first sight suddenly become obscure when one tries to translate them into a Western language, any of which compels one to make definite choices at every turn. The following footnote to a passage in the *Huai-nan Tzu*, which forms the basis for note 3 on p. 111, will serve as an illustration. The passage itself reads: "When Ning Ch'i sang a song (songs?) of Shang under (his?) cart, Duke Huan awoke with a sigh", which the commentator explains as follows:

Ning	Ning	When Ning Ch'i was
Ch'i	Ch'i	feeding the oxen
fan	feed	(his ox?) under
niu	ox (oxen?)	(his? a?) cart
ch'e	cart	(carts?),
hsia,	under,	
k'ou	knock	he sang a song
chioh	horn	(songs?) of Shang
Shang	Shang	while beating
ko.	sing.	(time) on their
Ch'i	Ch'i	horns (a horn?).
Huan	Huan	(Hearing him sing)
kung	Duke	Duke Huan of Ch'i
wu	awake-to	had a sudden insight
chih,	him,	(into his character)
yung	use	and (subsequently)
i	for	made him a
wei	be	Minister (at his
hsiang.	Minister	court).

Here the translation into any Western language *must* say ox or oxen, song or songs, horn or horns. As for the verbs, since it is a question of an ancient story, they must all be rendered in the past, but the question is by no means always so simple.

But if simple, straightforward, and even explanatory prose like the above is so lacking in clarity and detailed exactness, Chinese verse must be said to be far more so. Verse in a language like Chinese, which is composed entirely of indeclinable monosyllables, can of course know nothing of metre as we know it. Since the words are all single syllables of more or less equal force, the only metric device possible is to count off the words in groups, and in fact most Chinese poetry written up to T'ao Ch'ien's time was written in lines consisting of four or five monosyllables each, the types being known as *ssu yen shih* (four-word poems) and *wu yen shih* (five-word poems). This restriction of the number of words to express a given thought often made it necessary to dispense with even such aids to exact expression as the language did possess; adverbs of time and indications of number and person (pronouns, etc.) that would normally have been expressed in prose were ruthlessly pruned away in verse, with the result that it is frequently necessary to read a poem several times before one can decide how to place it, as it were, with regard to tense, number of persons involved, and so on. Sometimes a whole poem can be rendered in the past or present equally well; for instance, the one on p. 94 could be translated in the past tense throughout.

> Dwelling in poverty
>   I had no human contacts,
> And at times forgot
>   the turning of the seasons.

Even the line containing the word "now" could be rendered:

> If I did not now
>   find my happiness,
> How was I to know
>   there would be years to come?

In this case it was not the presence of the adverb "now", but the feeling of the poem as a whole which made me decide on the present tense.

The poem "On Moving House" (p. 60) is interesting in that it forces the use of three tenses in translation: the past tense while the poet describes how he had been looking forward to moving; the present, to describe the moving itself; the future, for the pleasures he expects to enjoy in his new home.

Hsi	Of old	
yü	wish	
chü	dwell	That I had long desired
nan	south	to dwell in the Southern village,
ts'un,	village,	

Fei	not	
wei	because	Was not because the house
po	divine	had been declared auspicious—
ch'i	the	[investigate by divination].
tse.	house.	

Wen	Hear	
to	many	Only that I had heard
su	plain	there were many plain-minded people
hsin	heart	
jen,	man,	

Lo	joy	
yü	with	With whom it were a joy
shu	count	to count the mornings and evenings.
ch'en	morning	
hsi.	evening.	

Huai	Cherish	
tz'u	this	I cherished the plan
p'o	rather	for quite a number of years,
yu	have	
nien,	year,	

Chin	now	
jih	day	But today at last
ts'ung	from	I am really moving house.
tz'u	here	
i	move	

Pi	Humble	
lu	hut	My modest dwelling
ho	why	why need it be large?
pi	necessarily	
kuang?	wide?	

Ch'ü	Take	
tsu	enough	Just so there is room
pi	cover	for my bed and mats.
ch'uang	bed	
hsi.	mat.	

156

Lin ⎫ ch'ü ⎬	Neighbours ⎫	⎫
shih	time	Neighbours and friends
shih	time	will come from time to time,
lai,	come, ⎭	⎭
k'ang	brave	⎫
yen	word	And with brave words
t'an	chat	we will talk of things of old.
tsai	at	
hsi.	old-time. ⎭	⎭
Ch'i	Rare	⎫
wen	text	Joyfully we will praise
kung	together	rare poetry together,
hsin	joyfully	
shang,	praise, ⎭	⎭
I	doubtful	⎫
i	meaning	And settle doubtful meanings
hsiang	mutual	by mutual discussion.
yü	with	
hsi.	explain. ⎭	⎭

Turning to the man-made or artificial difficulties of translation, we find the chief one is the habit of literary allusion. T'ao Ch'ien is exceptionally easy to translate because he is very sparing in his allusions, and those he does employ can all be detected and explained without difficulty. In the poems of later authors, however, we find verse after verse which would be impossible to translate without a footnote to explain virtually every other word.